A GENERATION MISSING

A GENERATION MISSING

BY CARROLL CARSTAIRS, M.C.

WITH A FOREWORD BY

OSBERT SITWELL

THE STRONG OAK PRESS
WITH
TOM DONOVAN PUBLISHING

A Generation Missing © William Heinemann Ltd
(First Published 1930)

Introduction & Chapter Notes
© The Strong Oak Press/Tom Donovan Publishing 1989

ISBN: 1-871048-02-8

Publishing History: This work was first published in 1930 and
has been out of print for many years. This edition reproduces
the original text complete and unabridged with the addition
of a new introduction and chapter notes.

Published by:
THE STRONG OAK PRESS LTD
with
TOM DONOVAN PUBLISHING LTD
PO Box 47
STEVENAGE
HERTS   SG2 8UH

Printed in Great Britain at The Bath Press, Avon.

Introduction to 1989 Edition

In the *Regulations for Recruiting for the Regular Army and the Special Reserve* current at the outbreak of war in 1914 the list of men "not to be allowed to enlist or re-enlist under any circumstances" included:

"(vi) A foreigner".[1]

This unequivocal exclusion had doubtless been set out in the Regulations to provide officers and N.C.Os. on recruiting duties with a simple and unambiguous response to any casually equiring foreigner.

In fact, both before and after the outbreak of war it was perfectly proper for any foreigner to enlist in the British army. The Army Act required only that the King "signify his consent through a Secretary of State" and that "the number of aliens serving together at any one time in any corps of the regular forces shall not exceed the proportion of one alien to every fifty subjects".[2] Nevertheless, the Act also stated that any alien "shall not be capable of holding any higher rank in His Majesty's regular forces than that of a warrant officer or non-commissioned officer". In short, to hold commissioned rank in the British army it was necessary to be a natural-born or naturalised British subject.[3]

There are no reliable statistics available to show how many foreign nationals were serving in the British army at the outbreak of war, or how many "friendly aliens" enlisted during the course of the war. However, there can be very little doubt that, while their country remained neutral, citizens of the United States made by far the largest proportion of this unlooked-for and welcome bonus of volunteers from overseas.[4]

One reason for the difficulty in reaching even an approximation of the numbers involved – and most especially for enlistments in the ranks – is the nature of the enlistments themselves. More often than not, and with complete disregard of the provisions of the Army Act, such enlistments required the deliberate falsification of the attestation paper, an operation that was usually achieved with the active connivance of the recruiter.

For example, when James Norman Hall, from Boston, presented himself at the Central London Recruiting Depot in Great Scotland Yard in August 1914 he was quite frank with the recruiting officers: "I admitted, rather boasted, of my American citizenship, but expressed my entire willingness to serve in the British army". After a brief conference with his colleagues a recruiting officer returned to say: "We'll take you, my lad, if you want to join. You'll just say you are an Englishman, won't you, as a matter of formality?"[5]

Arthur Guy Empey, from New Jersey, crossed to England to enlist when it became apparent that America was not going to declare war on Germany following the sinking of the *Lusitania*. The first recruiting officer turned down Empey's offer "as it would be a breach of neutrality", but having heard Empey's statement that "I am an American, not too proud to fight, and want to join your army", a second officer responded, "That's all right, we take anything over here".[6]

Other American volunteers included William J. Robinson and R. Derby Holmes. Robinson found himself adrift in London in September 1914 when his employers went bankrupt and he apparently had no difficulty in enlisting in the cavalry. Holmes signed on in Boston as a horse minder aboard the s.s. *Cambrian* transporting remounts to Britain. Many intending volunteers used this route as a means of reaching the war and it became a point of dispute between the American and British governments, especially when the volunteers were under age.

On reaching London in March 1916 Holmes also went to the Great Scotland Yard Recruiting Depot where he too was told that the British army did not accept neutrals. However, under the tutelage of a friendly recruiting sergeant he returned the next day, claimed he was a Canadian and was duly enlisted.[7]

For an American wishing to obtain a commission, the whole process seems to have been remarkably similar to enlistment in the ranks, except that it was a little more leisurely and gentlemanly. It appears that once again the most obvious disguise of nationality was also the most effective and it is probable that Americans applying for commissions tended to follow the course adopted by Carroll Carstairs and became "temporary" Canadians.[8]

Carroll Chevalier Carstairs was born in Philadelphia on 20th March 1888. He graduated from Yale in 1913 and in the autumn of that year joined the art dealers M. Knoedler and Company for whom his father, Charles S. Carstairs, acted as London representative.[9] By the summer of 1914 he had been working with his father in London for four months and when war broke out he was just returning from a buying trip to France. His "growing partisan mood" quickly led him to accept an invitation to join an "impromptu corps" (actually the embryo Intelligence Corps) then being formed to provide "scouts, guides and liaison officers", but his lack of German just as quickly disbarred him from accompanying them overseas. Although he had been "complete with uniform, booted and spurred, with sword at hip and all the rest of the paraphernalia" there is no record of his having been officially enlisted or commissioned at this time.

Carstairs was eventually commissioned as a temporary Second Lieutenant in the Royal Artillery on 14th December 1914 and according to the Monthly Army List for January 1915 he was posted to the 9th Divisional Ammunition Park, attached to the 9th Divisional Artillery. This appears to have acted briefly as a holding unit for newly commissioned Royal Artillery officers and by the beginning of February all these officers had been posted away, with

Carstairs listed as serving 3A Reserve Brigade, R.F.A., then stationed at Hilsea, near Portsmouth.

Early in 1915 Divisional Ammunition Parks started to reform as Army Service Corps units and No. 132 Company, A.S.C., was formed in January 1915 as the 9th Divisional Ammunition Park. The War Establishment of each Ammunition Park called for an officer of the Royal Artillery to be attached "for care of ammunition" and Carstairs joined 132 Company as their attached officer. They started to cross to France on 10th May 1915 and Carstairs disembarked at Rouen from the s.s. *Woodfield* with the "remainder of [the] vehicles" on 12th May.

The Park moved via Abbeville and Journy to Meteren which it reached on 18th May. On 7th June it moved to St. Venant and thence to Auchel on 26th June where the 9th Division joined I Corps and the Park became Corps Troops. Carstairs left the following day and on 28th June joined A Battery, 50th Artillery Brigade, 9th Division, at Bourecq. The Division's first major action was their assault on Fosse 8 on the first day of the Battle of Loos, 25th September 1915 and Carstairs begins the narrative of his Western Front service a day or so later by which time he appears to have been transferred to D/50 Battery.

Carstairs remained with the Division until November 1915 when he was transferred to the Grenadier Guards and returned to London on being posted to their 5th (Reserve) Battalion at Chelsea Barracks. His next move was not until September 1916 when he went back to France to join the 3rd Battalion Grenadier Guards (2nd Guards Brigade, Guards Division).

The 3/Grenadier Guards had landed in France on 27th July 1915 and on 19th August had joined the 2nd Guards Brigade at Esquerdes to become part of the newly formed Guards Division. The battalion had gone on to serve in the Battle of Loos, had held front line sectors near Laventie and in the Ypres Salient during the Winter of 1915 and the Spring and Summer of 1916 before moving south to the Somme front in August. It was heavily engaged in the initial assault of the Battle of Flers-Courcelette on 15th September and lost 17 officers and 395 other ranks killed and wounded. The battalion was relieved on 16th September and on 20th September moved into bivouacs at Carnoy where it was in reserve during the successful Guards Division capture of Lesboeufs on 25th September. Carstairs joined them the following evening as they prepared to move up to Trones Wood in support of the 1/Scots Guards and 2/Irish Guards then holding the front line. He first entered the front line with the 3/Grenadier Guards on 28th September 1916 when the battalion took over the line just north of Lesboefs from 1/Scots Guards.

Carstairs served with the battalion for a total of eleven months between September and December 1916, August 1917 and January 1918 (winning a Military Cross at Bourlon Wood in November 1917) and finally between August and November 1918. On 4th November 1918 he was very

severely wounded (the battalion lost 6 officers and 109 men killed, wounded and
missing that day) and remained in hospital
for several months. Duff Cooper, a fellow
officer, later recalled that Carstairs was
crippled for life.[11]

On his eventual return to America Carstairs reactivated his links with Knoedler
and Co. and in 1928 he was one of a group
of four, including his father, that purchased
the Knoedler business. When his father
died some six years later he left Knoedler
to establish a gallery bearing his own name
on New York's East Fifty-seventh Street,
and continued to make frequent buying
trips to Europe. He was regarded as one
of the leading American authorities on
modern painting and at the time of his
death his private collection is said to have
included a number of "masterpieces of the
French impressionist school".

Apart from *A Generation Missing* he also
published a small collection of verse, *My
Window Sill* (London, Heinemann, 1930),
and a volume of appreciations of various

artists, *Postscript to Criticism* (London, Seely Service, 1934).

Carroll Chevalier Carstairs died suddenly in Doctors Hospital, New York, on 2nd October 1948. He was 60 years old.

Peter T. Scott
November, 1988

NOTES

1 *Regulations for Recruiting for the Regular Army and the Special Reserve*, (London, War Office/H.M.S.O., 1912), para. 90. This edition was later reprinted with amendments to 31st August 1914.

2 Army Act, Section 95(1). Under the provisions of this section the King gave blanket approval to all future enlistments of the "subjects of allied nations" on 25th May 1916. By the time this consent had been translated into an Army Council Instruction (A.C.I. 1156/1916, 8th June 1916) the classification had been broadened to mean "friendly

aliens", a term later defined by the War Office as meaning "all aliens other than enemy aliens".

The overall 2 per cent proportion appears to have remained in force throughout the war, but the numbers in individual units such as the Middlesex (Aliens) Labour Companies and the Russian Labour Companies were not restricted to that percentage.

See: Public Record Office, Kew: WO32/4773; *Registration and Recruiting*, (London, [War Office], August 1916), pp. 20–23; A.C.I. 91/1916; A.C.I. 2047/1916; A.C.I. 859/1918. For wartime control of aliens see the Aliens Restriction Act, 1914.

3 *Registration and Recruiting* (pp. 20–21) defined a natural-born British subject as:

(a) Every person born in H.M. Dominions or on board a British ship, whatever the nationality of his parents may be:

(b) Every person born out of H.M.

Dominions, whose father or paternal grandfather was a natural-born subject by birth in H. M. Dominions.

4 In conversation with the American Assistant Secretary of State on 4th August 1916, Sir Cecil Spring-Rice, the British Ambassador in Washington, freely admitted that he "did not know how many Americans were serving in the British and French armies". (Public Record Office, Kew: F0115/2015). However, James M. Beck, in his foreword to Harry E. Brittain's *From Verdun to the Somme: An Anglo-American Glimpse of the Great Advance*, (New York, Lane, 1917), p. ix, claimed that 16,000 United States citizens had enlisted in the Canadian Expeditionary Force (*excluding* those who falsified their nationality) and that a further 10,000 had volunteered for active duty with French forces. In his *The American Volunteers with the Allies*, (Paris, Editions de "La Nouvelle Revue", 1918), p. 169, Paul-Louis Hervier quotes an

estimate of 5th April 1917 (the day
before America declared war on Germany) that 32,000 Americans "had
served or were serving in the English
and Canadian armies".

5 James Norman Hall, *Kitchener's Mob:
The Adventures of an American in the British Army*, (London, Constable, 1916),
pp. 3–4. Hall had been on a walking
tour of North Wales when war was declared. He enlisted in the 9/R. Fusiliers
(36th Bde., 12th Div.) and served with
them on the Western Front as a
machine-gunner. Following his discharge from the British army (a course
urged on the British Ambassador by
Senator Henry Cabot lodge on behalf
of Hall's parents) he returned to America where *Kitchener's Mob* first appeared
in the *Atlantic Monthly* between March
and May 1916. Hall later joined the
Escadrille Lafayette and in May 1918
he was shot down behind German lines
and remained a prisoner of war until
the Armistice.

The British Embassy in Washington received numerous appeals for the discharge of Americans who had volunteered for the British and Canadian armies. Where minors were involved every effort was made to locate and repatriate the young volunteers, often against their will. However, by December 1916 and in those cases involving adults, the British Ambassador was replying to appeals: "His Majesty's Government have ruled that they will not discharge foreigners of full age who enlist of their own free will in the British Army". Sir Cecil Spring-Rice to Congressman L. C. Dyer, 5th December 1916. (Public Record Office, Kew: F0115/2015).

6 Arthur Guy Empey, *From the Fire Step: The Experiences of an American Soldier in the British Army*, (London, Putnam, 1917), pp. 14–15. Empey appears to have been enlisted in either the 1/London or 3/London (167th Bde., 50th Div.) and then to have served with the

167th Brigade Machine Gun Co. until he was severely wounded during a raid on Gommecourt Park shortly before 1st July 1916. *From the Fire Step* (published in America as "*Over the Top*") was the most popular of all the narratives written by American volunteers with the B.E.F. and remained in print in America until the mid-1960s.

As for "neutrality", an American citizen was deemed to have invalidated his citizenship by swearing allegiance to a foreign country in order to serve in its army. When America entered the war the Congress passed an act whereby such citizenships could be re-acquired by simply swearing an oath of allegiance before a properly constituted authority.

7 William J. Robinson, *My Fourteen Months at the Front: An American's Baptism of Fire*, (London, Hodder and Stoughton, 1916). Robinson enlisted in the 5th Dragoon Guards and served in France from October 1914 to December 1915 before being discharged. R. Derby

Holmes, *A Yankee in the Trenches*, (Boston, Little, Brown, 1918). Holmes enlisted in the 22/London, served in France, was wounded and gained his discharge in May 1917.

Many other Americans who served in the British, Candian and French forces are noticed in Paul-Louis Hervier, *The American Volunteers with the Allies* (see note 4, above), Edwin W. Morse, *The Vanguard of American Volunteers in the Fighting Lines and in Humanitarian Service, August 1914 – April 1917*, (New York, Charles Scribner's, 1918) and F. A. Mackenzie, *Americans at the Front* (London, Hodder and Stoughton, 1917) which is also of interest as one of the British Government's Wellington House covert propaganda productions.

8 At least one American, Harry Butters, appears to have gained his commission in the 11/R. Warwickshire through the personal influence of the masters of Beaumont College, the school he had

attended in England, with an old boy of the school, Major C. G. Fuller, at the War Office. Butters later transferred to the R.F.A. and was killed in action on 31st August 1916. See: Mrs Denis O'Sullivan, ed., *Harry Butters, R.F.A. "An American Citizen"*, (New York and London, John Lane, 1918).

9 Charles S. Carstairs lived at No. 3 Chesterfield Street and the M. Knoedler & Co. Gallery was at 15A Old Bond Street.

10 Authority to form A.S.C. companies for the Divisional Supply Columns and Ammunition Parks of the New Armies was first given in A.C.I. 254/1914 and was confirmed by 20/A.S.C./794/ Q.M.G.3d on 11th January 1915. When 132 Co. became Corps Troops on 26th June 1915 its title was changed to 9th Ammunition Sub Park. It was absorbed by 131 Co. (9th Divisional Supply Column) on 13th March 1918.

11 Alfred Duff Cooper, Viscount Norwich, *Old Men Forget*, (London, Hart-Davis, 1953), p. 90.

ACKNOWLEDGEMENTS

My most grateful thanks go to: Victoria
Reed in North Carolina and Tom Gudmes-
tad in Seattle for their help in locating bio-
graphical information; Nancy C. Little
(Librarian/Archivist, M. Knoedler & Co.,
Inc.) in New York and Major (Retd.) E.
C. Weaver, M.B.E. (Regimental Archivist,
Grenadier Guards) in London for respond-
ing to my enquiries; Penny Swannell,
George L. Lawson and John Kasmin in
London for their valuable advice and assist-
ance; Jaqi Clayton for her help in London
and New York; the staffs of the Depart-
ment of Printed Books, Imperial War
Museum, and the Public Record Office,
Kew, for their unfailingly cheerful help.

Extracts from Crown Copyright material
in the Public Record Office appear by per-
mission of the Controller of H.M. Statio-
nery Office.

P.T.S.

To

"THE GENERATION AFTER"
who, with a change in the time-
table of the world's events, might
have lived these pages

AUTHOR'S NOTE

I hope the people whose names I have mentioned won't mind. I hope those whose names I have not mentioned won't mind!

Content

Foreword

A Generation Missing is an interesting book
in that it is true. We feel it to be true.
The faults we can find in it are not faults
in the book, but in the author. With the
exception of the " Prologue," which has the
real power of imagination, of symbolism,
as against emotionalism, the war is taken
emotionally. Now since the war was felt
in this way by an enormous majority, this
book is by that much more true to general
experience. In some ways to feel the war
emotionally, rather than intellectually, was
of benefit ; for it supplied an anodyne to
the intense suffering that would have been
caused by independent thinking. But emotion, or emotionalism, is the most persuasive, if maudlin, of recruiting sergeants,
even more persuasive than the mob instinct.

And it was the emotionalism of every side
that prolonged the war, and by so doing
ensured that every nation except America
should lose it; for the virtuous hysteria
which everyone cultivated made common-
sense appear shameful and earthy, so that
when a touch of it broke out in ourselves,
we quickly suppressed it, when in others
(as in the famous Lansdowne letter) exe-
crated it, and covered the person who had
let so unwelcome a spirit loose with
obloquy. Yet sooner or later, in spite of
every effort of statesmen, generals, newspaper proprietors, and club colonels, common-sense insists on a hearing. The great
"war-bogeys" such as Lloyd George,
Clemenceau, Bottomley and the rest of them,
are once more assessed at their true value.
Gradually the world ceased to see the
Russian troops passing through England,
ceased to believe that those who thought
war silly were, of necessity, German spies;
and though this undoubtedly makes life less
interesting for those who took no active
part in the war, yet it tends to make it a

little more comfortable for those who par-
ticipated and still survive.

Even now, however, the war is regarded as sacrosanct by the weight of its
own silliness ; that is to say, the appalling
misery inflicted by the imbecility of it is
held to make it something grand and good ;
and to question its practical politics (which
after all must be regarded at that level) to
question whether it was really necessary,
whether Britain had to enter, and whether
it would not have been wiser to prevent,
rather than encourage, the United States
from coming to the aid of the Allies, is still
considered as a form of blasphemy. Therefore one would like to see, even in war-
books, such as *All Quiet on the Western
Front*, a little more contempt and scorn, as
well as hatred, for the war. For next time,
should the necessity arise, let us, especially
those of us who have been soldiers, use
our heads, trust our heads : and the heart
of the world will benefit.

Apart from its general bearing, this book
interests me because the author and myself

served in the same regiment, and I find, in
reading him, that our impressions of it are
much the same. The great courtesy and
fairness of the senior officers, combined with
their insistence, when on duty, on discipline,
is that which most struck him. And it is
that, combined with a really fine old tradi-
tion, which has made the Brigade of Guards
the most efficient, as it is the most pleasant
in which to serve, of all units. The discipline there never seems to kill tolerance :
and this in spite of the fact that the soldier's
profession in peace time is not one which
usually attracts men of very wide mental
interests. Moreover, these soldiers were
able to see jokes against themselves and
remain amused. A year or so before the
war, for example, I remember a large dinner
at which were present several distinguished
officers. Some other general was referred
to, and a young officer, without thinking,
remarked, " Oh, he's an old fool," and when
requested to give his reasons for such a
statement, replied, " Well, if he wasn't one,
he wouldn't have stayed in the army long

enough to be a general!" And yet this
naïve answer was received with laughter.

Finally, to touch on controversial topics,
I wish to state, in spite of the protests of
those who believe in war, that war is the
friend, aider and abettor of such things as
venereal disease and drink. The army is not
and never has been, as the friends of war
pretend, a kind of annex to the Y.M.C.A.
The great increase in venereal diseases could,
of course, have been prevented to a great
extent : but the bishops and present-day
morality would not allow it, and the health
of thousands of men were ruined in conse-
quence. But to please the religious, the
sinner must suffer ; for if he did not, the sin
might cease to exist. As for drink, I have,
during the war, seen an infinite number of
all ranks who were drunk—and have always
deeply sympathised with them. . . . Here
again, perhaps, common-sense might be
allowed to enter in ?

OSBERT SITWELL.

Prologue

A SMALL boy, eight years old, sitting cross-
legged on the floor of his nursery, surveyed
a panorama of his own creation.   The worn
and faded green of a carpet (which in the
circumstances suggested a severe drought)
held the bright and serried ranks of two
opposing armies.   Little lead soldiers, taken
that Christmas morning out of their cardboard boxes and painstakingly placed in
their present positions by this higher agency,
faced each other in attitudes decreed by
their particular manufacturers. Some stood
to attention, others with arms sloped were
on the march, while others still with fixed
bayonets were prepared to meet a cavalry
charge.   The boy wore a puzzled frown.
Having got his tiny puppets into battle
array, how was he to conduct the battle?

1

He regarded his men doubtfully—the eye
of destiny itself for a moment baffled. They
presented a motley though a colourful appearance. There were Guardsmen in bearskins
and scarlet tunics, and Royal Fusiliers in
khaki. Ghurkas in turbans and American
Indians in warpaint and feathers. United
States troops in blue with dark-skinned
Cubans in white. French Zouaves in baggy
red trousers stood between Italian Bersag-
lieri in green, and kilted Highlanders. There
was even a company, garbed as for a fancy
dress ball, in the uniform of the eighteenth
century—pike and shako and scarlet coatee.
There were lancers with pennants of red
and white, and Prussian Uhlans in peaked
helmets. A few cannon concealed in a
wood, whose trees were the exact replica of
those in a " Douanier " Rousseau, and some
houses of painted stucco completed the
picture.

The boy's idea of battle was not disso-
ciated from death and destruction. But
how inflict casualties so that each was decided not by the boy but by fate alone ? How

deal them out fairly? "Deal" suggested something. Cards! He ran to find his mother.

She was in the library, a book on her lap, but she was not reading. She was tired; a reaction to the nervous energy and sympathy put into her son's enjoyment of Christmas.

"Mother!" he cried, "can I have a pack of cards?"

"What for?" (Why do parents invariably question and why are children invariably secretive?)

"Oh, nothing, Mother. Can I?"

"Yes, of course." She rose and went to a desk. Opening a drawer, she selected a used pack. "Here you are, dear."

"Thank you, Mother." He was off immediately. His mother followed, but not at once.

In the nursery, presiding over his miniature armies, he soon had the battle under way. Fortune herself determined its course. As one side opened fire the cards were dealt and a card placed before each man fired at.

A face card and he was a casualty. An ace he was killed; a king and he was seriously, perhaps mortally, wounded (a black card following and he died—a red and he recovered). A queen and he was wounded and out of action. A knave and he was wounded but might still go on fighting if he had the pluck. (A card was then dealt to determine this—a diamond or heart and he continued despite his wound and thereby earned a decoration.) Any other than a face card and the man escaped.

So it went. The boy decided attack and counter-attack, but fate determined success or failure. Except where the cannon were concerned; from these he fired little pellets, pulling back the spring himself—so many shots a side. Sometimes his governess fired for the enemy, but she was so indifferent a shot that he had to give her up. Once the cannon inflicted considerable damage. The soldiers being in close order, the man hit took the whole line with him in his fall.

After several battles, the boy noticed one

young officer who bore a charmed life. Card after card had been dealt him without his even receiving so much as a knave. Scatheless he passed through battle after battle. The boy grew to identify this young subaltern with himself. Not consciously, but vaguely. He became a symbol, a presage, a premonition. When it finally became his turn to be dealt a card the boy became pink with excitement and anticipation. Once, peeping, he expected an ace which happily turned out to be a two.

Not until the late spring, when the family were about to leave New York for England, did the young officer receive his face card— a king. Seriously, perhaps mortally, wounded in a charge at the head of his men !

The little boy sat lost in thought, wishing he could take back the card or hand it to another man. Somehow he could not ; he was instinctively honest. And besides, the fact would remain no matter what he did. But the card following—the black card that meant death or the red card that meant life ?

5

He could not bring himself to turn that card up.

He put away his toy soldiers, back into their boxes, into the little niches made for each man.   He put them all away and never played with them again.

*   *

*

Chapter I

I

2m.   Edition Speciale : 5 centimes

LE PROGRÈS

*L'Angleterre déclare la Guerre à l'Allemagne
La Nation est en Danger*

FAISONS NOTRE DEVOIR

and in the following page (such a French touch) " Avis-L'Epicerie Potin n'augmente pas les Prix de ses Marchandises," on the very same page " Il est mort pour la France et pour l'humanité (l'humanité ! !)—C'est exactment le 3 août à 5 heures 45 du soir que la guerre a été declarée.   Nous n'avons plus à souhaiter maintenant que la victoire de nos armées," etc.

This edition of Le Progrès, now fifteen years old, which had remained, through change and time, in my possession, was now

7

before me. I could recreate but dimly and in miniature, as it were, the emotion of that day in Le Havre when I had excitedly perused its pages. Its paper had yellowed with age, its tone was autumnal ; the bold type with its astonishing news stood out at the end of fifteen years strangely futile and fantastic.

Let me project myself into the past. I am sitting again not so much in the restaurant as in the centre of tremendous and trans-fixing events, and my thoughts are not on the half million dollars worth of uninsured paintings in the hold of *La France*. The steamer might or might not sail ; it might or might not be sunk ; somehow the possibility did not touch me, for I was young, and there was a war on whose growing pro-portions looked like including any youth with a decent pulse.

No, my thoughts were not on the pictures. I was watching again the young French officer pointing with a laugh at his closely cropped head. The pretty young girl whom he was addressing laughed too. But their laughter had that peculiar note that kept one

8

from joining in—a quality of restraint and of bravado.

That night I returned to Southampton. We were requested to show our passports—" excepté les Anglais." I resented the completely unintentional slur cast on my growing partisan mood. And when, on the way from Southampton to London, an English girl proclaimed that were she a man, she would enlist, I felt her remark somehow included me. . . .

2

The war was on and I was in. Who can trace to its original source the yielding to an impulse of this sort? What is the background of an act? For now that I had " joined " I seemed to have done it automatically, an action reflex to things long dreamt about and dwelt upon; visions of old battles, stories of ancient combat, tales of romance and chivalry without number, which had intrigued me since childhood. These dream rivulets had flowed out into the wide ocean of reality. The step was

9

predestined, the result of a long fascination.

I was " part of it all "—a vague phrase which linked one with one's fellowmen and left one feeling miserably alone. Where was the exaltation that should have risen like a spiritual rocket from the dying embers of a discarded life ? I had the sensation not of taking on something new but of everything falling away from me. There was a tightening at the throat of nerves and muscles that seemed to connect directly with the pit of the stomach. The habit of living, as I had known it, had been abruptly and completely broken off, terminated by myself. The war, as far as England was concerned, was but a day old. Volunteers had not been called for. And besides, I was an American.

To my father I said, " Well, I have got a lot out of life." He might have replied " You have not begun to live," but he remained quiet, gazing out of the motor at the shifting scene of a London street. I myself felt no stimulus from my brave speech. It had slipped out ready-made, cut to the boy's preconceived attitude toward war. . . .

I awoke early the next morning to the full choir of birds outside my window, and leaving my bed I peered out over the trim lawn. How tremulously day broke to their pretty and concerted chirruping. I wished I knew more of birds. Robin I knew and wagtail—dimly I was aware that ever since the step taken the day before I had been continuously fastening on things outside myself.

The familiar noise of a waking house greeted my ears ; the sound of a dustpan against the wood of a broom, the tread of a step, the shutting of a door. It was time to shave and dress and then there would be breakfast. The day was beginning and ushering in the customary round inseparable from existence. There was comfort in this.

I found my father unusually restrained. His eyes had brightened overnight. I felt a pang for my father. He had begun to count on me, to think of me as securely fixed. I felt an impulse to go and put my arm around him and say something. The impulse grew to an emotion. He made a simple observation and the emotion died away.

I was looking out of the window. From where I sat I could see the fine copper beech half way down the lawn. I loved that tree. I formulated the thought " I love that tree." I was instinctively recording objectives : birds, trees, the smell of the lilies that were always in the front hall—they would be the kind of things to think about for happiness in the future.

I stood in the front hall waiting for my father—an act which it was difficult to accept had about it the element of dread finality. . . .

3

Suddenly, for so it seemed, although the respectable passage of another day had intervened, I found myself in a railway carriage, complete with uniform, booted and spurred, with sword at hip and all the rest of the paraphernalia, swaying swiftly forward to the unknown, to the incredible, to the fantastic—to war. A week before I had been peacefully studying in the British Museum, itself a veritable sanctuary of peace, its very existence the outcome of a multitude of peaceful lives following peaceful pursuits. Transition indeed ! . . .

We were on the outskirts of Southampton and " under canvas." Now that I was definitely placed I found myself wondering how it had come about that I was here. In the light of the past I stood revealed as by a conjurer's trick, a gigantic sleight-of-hand. The step that had brought it about had been big enough, heaven knows, but the mental processes that should have accompanied it, stage by successive stage, had been left far behind. I felt light-headed, as though, whirled through space, I had been abruptly set down. I had the where-am-I feeling of waking amidst new surroundings. I sensed my body separate from my soul ; functioning separately, my mind astray. I had lost my sense of identity, that sense of secure identity which attends the daily habit of repeating this and that and which is derived from a continuity of familiar sound and touch and sight and smeli. People would think my being here the result of my own initiative, an act of courage. On the contrary, I had been carried along on the crest of the world's event, that was all. It was weakness, the inability to resist the tide of time. No, it was not weakness ; it was youth. The flow of warm young blood that catches us in its current and takes us along into the channels of adventure, romance. . . . I discovered the day had gone to the performance of duties with which the mind had been only mildly associated. A thousand memories kept cropping up, countless episodes of childhood and boyhood that came and went apropos of nothing. They formed a bulwark against loneliness. I had not known such acute nostalgia since that first day I was left at school by my mother, now dead these seven years. (I remember catching cold shortly after and hoping I would become ill enough to be sent home.) A man adrift in a boat might be affected in a like manner. There was that about it, a feeling of being launched into space, into infinity, rudderless, at the mercy of ebb and flow. I was like a man blindfolded who could see light only at his feet. No longer would they move actuated by any impulse of my own. Life seemed at the point of complete frustration.

The ground in my tent gave forth the condensed smell of earth in a flower pot. The light of a single candle threw strange shadows on my bell-shaped tent. Time being what it was, even shadows had become distorted !

In the afternoon I watched a battalion of infantry swing past, singing, "It's a long way to Tipperary." It was one of many battalions detraining and embarking for the front. Southampton was the bottle-neck through which England poured her regular army into France. What amazed me was the calm with which the population received those fighting men. Have the long Napoleonic wars bequeathed this coast line, so accustomed to war, an inheritance of stoic resignation ? I myself was thrilled. At the time of the Spanish-American war I was eight years old. I remember it indistinctly, but something of the emotion it generated within me has remained astir throughout all the subsequent years. I returned to camp with a lighter step. I felt those marching, singing men at my elbow.

As I walked into camp, I was told to report to the orderly room.

Major Harrington addressed me kindly. It was he who had been responsible for taking me into this impromptu corps. Hurriedly organised by some ex-cavalry officers, its members to act as scouts, guides and liaison-officers, it had received an all too hasty recognition from a busy War Office.

I vaguely grasped what he said. I was not to go; they were very sorry, but it was essential that all should speak German. They were awfully nice about it—it had nothing to do with them, a telegram from the W.O., they added. Of course, I would find something else with no difficulty. I left, outwardly cursing my luck while an inward flow of joy suffused my whole being. I was mortified at this reaction. I should have felt righteous indignation. I continued to appear

16

crestfallen though feeling a hypocrite when several commiserated with me.

" Never mind," said one, " you'll find plenty of things in London. Most of us will have our toes in the daisies before long."

The Adjutant approached.

" You must turn in all Government equipment."

To the annoyance of everyone in the Corps we had been handed out rifles. A day after we had moved camp and I had left behind my rifle.

The Adjutant looked incredulous. " Good God, man, that's a military crime! Go fetch it."

A walk of half a mile brought me to the site of the camp so recently evacuated. There was the circular patch of ground my tent had covered, already discoloured owing to its brief confinement; and there, too, the rifle. After all, who would have taken it? I hastily retraced my steps and delivered up the precious piece of Government property. Someone else would use it now. I said farewell to two or three and as I left Julian

17

Martin Smith called out " Bad luck ! "   I
thought of this a month later when I heard he
had been killed.   I thought, too, of the forty
pounds he had started out with, twenty to
spend on the way and twenty to spend in
Berlin.

Waterloo Station at the moment of my
arrival about nine p.m. was quite empty ; a
porter or two, a traveller or two, and that was
all. A lone taxi stood in the rank. It gave me
an odd feeling of triumphant escape to tell
the chauffeur where to go and have him act
on my bidding. I pulled the strap to allow the
window to slip gently down, and peered into
the night.   Where was everybody ?   The
streets were deserted. London, I discovered,
had a strange way of looking quite unin-
habited. London actually rested at night. It
made me feel relaxed. Or was I tired ? The
reaction ! Those four busy days with battle in
the offing and now on the way home at night
and in uniform as though returning from a
masquerade. That's it, a masquerade ! Pierrot
poor fool, thought he could play a serious
part.

The taxi turned in at the gate and its
wheels made a crunching noise along the
driveway. I sprang out and paid the man,
helping him haul off my big Wolseley valise,
anxious to have him go before someone in
the house should enquire into this unex-
pected sound of a motor. After we had got
the valise near the door I rang the bell and
thought of the scent of the lilies in the hall
that would soon greet my nostrils.

At sight of me the butler's face betrayed a
look of comic astonishment. It changed
like a face of wet putty into which you had
suddenly stuck your finger. "Hush," I
whispered, and while Graves still wore the
same startled look, I turned from him with
the impression that he had changed his
expression for good. From now on he'd
look startled and I'm responsible. Coin-
cidentally I reflected "What a funny thing to
think about."

4

I lay with my eyes closed and my mind
actively at work. The early light peeped into

my curtained room and the birds chirped and
warbled as they had done that other morning,
only now without significance. I woke to the
realisation that the relief I had felt at my
release had been momentary, was indeed
fragmentary, having nothing to do with the
thing as a whole, and I lay pondering over it.
I had been *freed*. But freedom is an affair of
the minute, it is a transition stage, it is the
little stretch of time and space that lies
between what you have done and what you
are to do. There is no *condition* of freedom.
Soon I should be taking on my old habits,
habits which would involve duties, duties
which would enslave once more.

At breakfast my father with a contented
look gave me instructions for the day.

I murmured, " All right, Father," resent-
ing ever so slightly the settled way in which
he returned to his paper. I thought a little
more interest in me, based on recent events,
would not have been out of place. I realised
all at once that I had shrunk immeasurably
since the day before, had visibly diminished to
a microscopic degree. Again I should be taken

for granted, left out of people's calculations.

Taking on the habits of my former existence, so briefly relinquished, should have come easily, but the relief I had experienced at being liberated, the actual joy of my homecoming, had given way to restlessness. The momentum transmitted by my incipient act stuck to me, drew me in its wake. I felt oddly committed.

Added to the personal equation there loomed the greater fact of national peril. I began to see myself outside of myself, as a man required to do his bit. I grew smaller, an atom receding into an ever-widening issue which would slowly encompass all. It would be impossible to view one's self as outside the scope of its influence. I was a man on the banks of a river at flood tide whose swift current was carrying everything before it, everything identified with youth. If I belonged not to England, I belonged to youth. Was I to forfeit forever the chance of championing its cause?

*　　　　　*

*

Chapter II

I

ALL Americans anxious to get into the war in 1914 frequented Mrs. Oliver's sitting-room at the Bentinck Hotel. Here drinks were served (and charged) to everyone. Others were present. There was the Nut—never quite sober and never quite drunk. There was Peter Donne who had lost an arm during the retreat from Mons. It took a great many whiskies to ease the continuous pain he had to bear. There were some that came and went—those on short leave from the front. I don't remember their names. One with whom I had talked, whose reactions I deemed might coincide with mine, I finally questioned.

" Would you like to be out of it ? "

" No," he replied thoughtfully. " You see all one's friends are out there."

He went out again, to remain forever with his friends : those who were killed !

Something of the excitement, the heightened spirit and energy generated by the war seemed to me concentrated in the small space created by the four walls of Mrs. Oliver's sitting-room. Through the clouds of cigarette smoke I could see myself in battle; a drink too much and I felt a reckless courage in the face of an imagined danger. During these lapses a word or a laugh near me, whose immediate significance was not quite understood, seemed like the encouragement and applause of my brother officers. I would leave the Bentinck with quite a swagger although I was not even in the army at the time.

Obtaining a commission in the British Army presented difficulties. Regulations had it that no one who was not a British subject could hold a commission in His Majesty's forces. One felt certain, however, that something would turn up and in the meantime merely to toy with the idea of going meant much. I used to say " I would like to get into something." I would speak carelessly as though joining a world war were to me a

23

thing of daily occurrence. I must say the man I happened to address looked intrigued. Going into a war such as this, if not impelled to, seemed to many rather extraordinary. Mrs. Oliver, however, took a personal interest in getting us all into the war.

" Here's Mr. Cardboard ! " (She never got my name right.) " Can't you get him into the Kentshires ? " As she invariably addressed the Nut who was invariably beyond grasping her meaning, I did not progress far. " We call him the Nut," she would end by saying.

I smiled approval, although I felt tempted to remaɪ ː that she was probably appealing to the person least capable of getting me into anything.

When at the end of a month I got a bill for ninety-seven pounds for cocktails, I gave up the Bentinck. There was another reason. Someone took me to the War Office. After writing on a form that I was born in Canada I was given a commission in the Royal Field Artillery.

That night I dined at the Savoy with Peter Donne. In those days officers not on

24

duty could wear plain clothes. A young officer in uniform passed our table. His arm was in a sling.

"Nasty bicycle accident I suppose," observed Peter Donne in a loud voice.

2

Shoeburyness, a small place at best, lay buried in darkness. Directly opposite Ostend (there were notices telling you where to fall in in the event of an air raid) and consequently somewhat an outpost in these war days, it was permitted but a scattered few dim lights.

Passing slowly from billet to officers' mess I felt in a bodily sense something of the town's own obliteration. As if in collaboration with the War Office itself, a single star twinkled shiftily in a sky of drifting clouds.

3

We were due to leave at almost any time. Spring had come and time again was wide-eyed. I felt its wistful beauty and its multiple life replenished me. As we clattered along the roads I imagined a sense of continuity as though at the end of the day's march lay the battle front already so close to my own horizon line.

4

I forgot the spring as I experienced again the substantial enjoyment of walking between houses in London streets. Each house was an invitation, because each suggested warmth and comfort and kindness and good cheer. Should I pass a house I knew I should certainly seek to enter. Put its familiar wall between me and my immediate future.

I took no taxi, I walked everywhere. In these early months of 1915 not all were in the masquerade and I for one felt a certain pride in my uniform. I stepped out with a measured stride, neither looking to the right nor left, but conscious, although I appeared not to be, of any glance in my direction. I imagined what people might be thinking.

" Smart young officer."

26

" I wonder if he is on leave from the front ? "

" Poor fellow, what danger he will face."

Such fancies, invested in others, bucked me up considerably. I felt very much more military than I had done in camp or on parade under the superior eye of a senior officer or the look of veiled sarcasm from an old sergeant.

Mrs. Oliver was much the same. After waiting a month to pay my bill I had been sent another for a hundred and seven pounds although I had not since set foot in her hotel. I had thereupon paid the first bill and destroyed the second. She did not seem to mind.

Beginning life as a cook, she had preserved a Cockney accent through thick and thin.

" Mr. Cardstairs ! " she exclaimed. (The name was correctly spelt on the bill.) " 'Ave a cocktile ? There's the Nut. We 'ad Oliver Filley here a while back. 'E's in the Flying Corps." (Filley had stroked a Harvard crew.)

27

She gave me all the news. Read, who had played in a Yale football team, was also an airman. " Dill " Starr, the Harvard all-American quarter-back, was in Gallipoli. The athletes are doing well, thought I, getting quite a kick at my close association with them. There were others. Walter Oakman, another Harvard man, had started in armoured motors, and Harold Fowler, who later joined the Gunners and then the Flying Corps. Arnold Whitridge (Yale) was in the " gunners." My brother Stewart had gone to France and joined the Foreign Legion. Anything I could do would seem commonplace by comparison.

The walls of Mrs. Oliver's room were draped with photographs of officers in uniform. Some had been serving when the war broke out, so that already several had been " killed in action." She pointed these out, giving each a name. She made death seem quite trivial. It was, and continued to be, and yet individually life remained precious.

Mrs. Oliver had a way of straying from

A GENERATION MISSING

one subject to another.

" Dorothy Lorne 'as been asking about
you.   She was 'ere the other day."

I had met Dorothy Lorne some months
before at a party in the Bentinck.   She was
slim and cool and impersonal.   At a time
when preoccupation with one's own life,
indeed with life itself, was instinctive, she
was peculiarly qualified to attract me.   I
wrote and she answered and yet there grew
no obligation on either side, and little
intimacy.

5

I had not let Dorothy know I was coming
to London on leave.   So that I was lucky
that afternoon to find her in.   She was a
self-sufficient young person.   Her sitting-
room with her piano and her music, her
books and her sewing, was her proper
setting and she adhered to it.

She was glad to see me.   Now that I had
the real Dorothy before me, instead of her
recollection, she took on, at least momen-
tarily, a certain colour and warmth.   Perhaps

it only appeared so because I had seen few women recently.

After a bit she picked up some needlework which kept her eyes averted, and that sense of detachment which was her charm, struck me anew.

It was a slight challenge too, and I said, " Sing me that thing of Quilter's to the poem by Ernest Dowson."

She rose at once.   She was always ready to sing.   Do I remember the words ?

" They are not long, the weeping and the
      laughter,
   Love and desire and hate ;
   I think they have no portion in us after
   We pass the gate.

   They are not long, the days of wine and
      roses ;
   Out of a misty dream
   Our path emerges for a while then closes
   Within a dream."

I forgot she was a vehicle for the song.

Merely the mouthpiece of its sentiment. I
felt the words strongly and the spell she
wrought in pronouncing them was such that
to fancy they came straight from her own
heart was easy. She lost her impersonal
quality when she sang. Her strong young
voice became a direct appeal and conveyed
the illusion that a new intimacy, a greater
sympathy existed between us.

I was very émotioné for a few minutes
after the song was finished. She had the
intuition to say nothing so that the magic
of the song lingered, a faint and intangible
intoxicant.

She let me take her in my arms and kiss
her. It meant nothing to her; she was
artist enough to make the moment supreme
for me.

" I love you."

She smiled.

" Why do you smile ? "

" Would you have me weep ? "

" I think I would. Hot tears. You are
so cold and self-contained. And yet I like
it. Why do I like it ? "

31

" You don't want to be implicated. That is why."

" Is that it ? "

She nodded.

" Women are so wise."

" Tell me about yourself."

" At least *you* are wise. You live for yourself, but charmingly. You ask nothing, you demand nothing, none of the thousand little exacting things women ask of men. And so quite suddenly one is ready to give you everything."

She laughed. " I said tell me about yourself. Why did you go into the war ? You are not warlike."

" Perhaps that's why. Like a letter that needs a stamp to get somewhere."

" To be torn up and thrown into a waste-paper basket—to be destroyed. It's not even your war."

I thought of one of the many catch words. " L'humanité ! "

" Tommy rot."

" Jolly old Tommy rot ! "

" Silly."

32

" Perhaps I shall be sorry. Perhaps I'm sorry now. I don't know. I'm not sufficiently formed to be anything. If the war lasts long I suppose it will get on one's nerves. If not it will create a background. People will say, ' he was in the war.' That will help me, won't it ? "

She did not reply. Somehow there seemed little else to say. I rose and took her hand. It lay limp in mine. Her eyes turned into doubtful stars.

" Good-bye," she said, " and that means, you know, ' God be wi' ye.' "

" Does it ? I didn't know. Good-bye then."

*   *   *   *

At the Bentinck a telegram awaited me.

" Bad news ? " asked Mrs. Oliver. A kindly person, I thought. Father was in the States. I conceived a sudden affection for Mrs. Oliver; she busied about the room, moving haphazardly hither and thither like a fly on a flat pool of water.

33

"It depends on the point of view." I handed her the telegram. This was a big moment in my life.

"So you're going out." Her voice was different and she turned away. "Don't forget that photograph you promised."

Would she be pointing it out one day saying, "I knew him well. Nice young American . . ."

*   *

*

Chapter III

I

THE Battery, which was in an enfilading position, had lost touch owing to a cut telephone wire. I was detailed to lay wire to a Brigade Headquarters. I began in the morning but it was not until early the next morning that I had completed my task. We started along a communication trench down which the wounded Scottish soldiers of the 9th Division were coming—minute particles of the attacking waves drifting back with the ebb of the tide. They moved along the trench, weary and dazed, and suffering silently, the spent and broken remnants of those first fine Kitchener battalions. It was impossible to recognise in them the men who had swung so lustily along the roads, behind the weird and plaintive, the almost prophetic wailing of their pipes. Some were being carried on stretchers, their ashen faces turned to the grey sky; others dragged along with gaping and bloody wounds, the lesser wounded helping the more helpless. Somehow I could hear again the low skirling of their pipes as, still under shell-fire, they crawled and shuffled away from their first murderous battlefield. . . . I gave one man a cigarette and he told me he had been in three bayonet charges the day before, and I thought the world should be draped in mourning for these mighty sufferers.

Soon it began to rain, a thin persistent rain. To make matters worse, the 7th Division, relieving the 9th, appeared coming up the trench; meeting the wounded coming down, the congestion became terrible. There was no room for me, and I and my signallers continued laying the wire on top of the trench, although the chances of the wire getting cut or, incidentally, our getting hit were greater. Up the trench I kept pace with the 7th regular Division—jaunty, doughty Cockneys who scoffed with grim but good-humoured sarcasm at the failure of Kitchener's volunteers, and who felt a kind of pride that they, the regulars, should have been needed. "We 'ad to be called on to finish their job for 'em," I heard one say. Poor devils, little did they reckon of the morrow's massacre that awaited them. But I did not see them the following morning—I think of them still cocky and sure and ready to tackle what they considered was their own professional job.

Day changing into night found us still carrying our reel of wire, slipping along ground that was rapidly becoming a morass. The rain, relentlessly continuing, blurred our vision so that we had to crawl along the very edge of the communication trench that we might not lose our way. Soaked to the skin (I had left my mackintosh behind), heavy with water and mud and weariness and lack of food (we had brought no rations) we moved along at a snail's pace. Our objective became an undreamed-of possibility. The men of the 7th, now silent or quietly cursing and dimly described in the night of rain, moved endlessly forward, choking the trench.

The dim light of a candle, pallid through the rain-soaked fissures of the curtained sand-bag entrance, denoted a dugout. I slithered up to its entrance as a Colonel (who I learned later was commanding the Brigade) appeared in its contracted doorway. He wedged me and my telephone into a crowded dugout next to his own and I got through to my Battery Commander.

To the tune of a new battle I was relieved the next day and towards noon got back to the Battery, utterly exhausted.

My servant met me (he had been Barton's and Barton was killed two days before).

" Get me some breakfast."

About the time he had reached the entrance of the officers' mess, I heard a shell. I had heard many shells. I paid no attention. I waited. Someone came in.

" Where the devil's my breakfast ? Where's Clark ? "

" Clark's dead. He was killed outright a few minutes ago. Didn't you hear the shell ? "

That he should have been killed while

performing a personal duty for me turned me
sick. I think I was sick. Then I went to
sleep and slept like a child—and a man had
been *killed* getting *my* breakfast and my bed
was the stretcher that carried his master,
Barton, to the divisional burying ground!
But one had to accept these things in a purely
matter-of-fact way—one had to accept everything as happening outside of oneself, like a
cab running over somebody else; there
could be no relation between cause and effect.

We were shelled from time to time—
" strays " meant for the road, which the men
cheerfully called souvenirs. We " slept " in a
cellar strengthened with sand-bags.

The battle of Loos rolled intermittently on.
I had ceased to wonder what was happening.
It had been accepted by everyone as dwindling away to a dismal failure. Mentally and
bodily, I was pinned to our own guns and to
their unceasing periodic barking. Sensation,
which rose gallantly and experimentally to
meet the high storm of battle, had become
pocketed. The divisional infantry, assem-
bling in handfuls behind the lines, had been

evacuated while its artillery lingered on,
hurling last minute missiles at the dead bodies
of their comrades, hanging on the uncut wire
or lying in the recaptured German trenches.

2

At the end of twelve days and nights the
Battery limbered up and creaked uneasily
away from the little village of Cuinchy.
Cuinchy with its one house still intact and its
population of one man and his grown-up
daughter, whom some were unkind enough
to consider as spies. I wonder how much
longer their house stood and what was their
fate. Did a chance shell get the father or
the daughter ? Did they crouch in the
cellar under some heavy bombardment,
their house tumbling about their ears, to
trudge wearily on to Béthune the next day ?
I should go back and find out.

Out of the local storm of battle we
clattered away, feeling more and more its
peculiar isolation as we penetrated the peaceful hinterland. Here the leaf fell from the tree
unhurried but by the autumn day's sharper

appetite. The women worked stolidly in the fields and the children played in the streets. Little heed was paid us as we entered with souls a shade darker into the village in which we were billeted.

We sat up late that night in the officers' mess, drinking.

" Did you hear about the carrier pigeon ? "

" No."

" The staff wanted to see how the old bird would work so it was given to an officer to take into a battle. He was supposed to write a message at a certain point giving his position—map reference and all. He detailed his orderly to carry it. You can imagine the orderly's point of view climbing in and out of shell holes, over and around obstacles, tripping over barbed wire with rifle, pack, gas mask and so forth and to crown all, a damned bird. He didn't like it much. But the bird did its duty. Flew back straight and true with a message tied to its leg. Great excitement on the part of the staff. Perfectly delighted ! What do you suppose the message said ? "

41

" I can't imagine."

" ' I'm tired of carrying this bloody bird'!"

" Did you hear about the man in the Camerons ? "

" No."

" Hit the morning of the first day of the attack as he jumped to the parapet—zero hour precisely. He was overheard saying, ' God damn those f——g Germans, they never gave me a chance.' "

" A sergeant in the Black Watch told me the Guards Division went in ' as though on parade.' "

The following day we took the road again and after a time were in the vicinity of Poperinghe and learned (I with a little awe) that we were going into the famous Ypres salient. Large drafts had again increased the Division to its normal size. Its new battalions marching the road took on the haunting look of the old. The salient, within its heated limits, soon seasoned raw material. There a soldier, if not a casualty, was a veteran in a few weeks.

I thought of this while the guns in the

salient were busy and the windows of the
officers' mess rattled gently like tea cups on
an express train.

3

On a very dark but tranquil night we
"took over" and the Battery went into
position behind a road which led directly into
Ypres. We messed in a partially wrecked
house and our sleeping quarters were in a
ruin, one room of which was draughtily
intact. At night, from officers' mess to billet,
I passed among rats so sluggish with over-
feeding that they were hardly able to get out
of one's way. In the trenches you saw them
skipping along the parapet silhouetted against
the sky. We found a rat trap and put it in our
sleeping room and one night I entered to a
frantic clanking noise. An enormous rat had
been caught by the hind leg and was leaping
up and down in a wild effort to get free. Coming up within a few feet of him, I drew my
revolver with a fiendish joy and shot him,
discovering afterwards that I had not

43

only killed the rat but broken the trap.

This was indeed a salient, and at night the enemy flares, seen at almost all points of the compass, gave one the illusion of being surrounded. Ypres itself was about a half mile away and as the day faded its jagged outlines took on the appearance of an enormous turreted and battlemented castle. I watched it often and with fascination, for its name meant much, and I resented the big shells that fell into it daily, levelling it more and more—although from this distance the seeing eye could scarcely record the change. From the first I conceived a secret desire to visit it and one day my curiosity was gratified. Passing between the houses of a city empty of life I felt more solitary than I had ever felt before. It was like visiting Pompeii. I had the sensation not that a myriad individual shells but that one giant upheaval had reduced this town to its abysmal proportions. I walked along its silent streets like an eavesdropper, marvelling at the minute detail of its destruction. Here the front of a house had been lifted away, like a great drop scene, revealing the intimate life within—beds and bureaus and tables, wardrobes and clothes and books remained as they had been left, like some huge doll's house awaiting the confusion of a final shattering blow.

My departure was punctuated by the bursting of a big shell behind me and as I looked around at the pall of black smoke drifting over the city, I thought the life of the Town Major of Ypres a most unpleasant one. I learned afterwards that "he" lasted a month. At the end of a month he had been killed, wounded, buried, shell-shocked, or owing to breakdown, evacuated.

4

Time, like a clock run down, dragged on, pulseless. Day succeeded day with a monotony that was varied by variations in a most variable climate. But autumn was crystalising into winter and more than one day had come with frost on the ground—a relief after days of pelting rain. Life was reduced to a routine of the utmost simplicity. One day was spent as Forward Observing Officer, one day on duty with the Battery, and the third off. On the third day one might remove one's clothes, get into a sleeping bag and rest —that is, if it was peaceful. Sometimes there took place a period of general " frightfulness " when one returned automatically to duty. As the cold increased the important point was whether we might or might not have a fire in the mess. A crack in the chimney, made by a shell splinter, made it possible only if the wind were from the right direction. Otherwise we sat, chill and ill-tempered, in a very uncomfortable room. We were occasionally shelled, and one still and beautiful day " Silent Sue " (so-called for the speed and soundlessness of this shell's approach) wounded one of our best signallers. The day was so lovely the casualty came with the shock of an accident.

We escaped, however, the dreadful hammering which " A " Battery, some five hundred yards in our immediate front and in full view of us, received. Given away by gun flashes seen by an aeroplane, it was

suddenly dealt the full thunderbolt of an
avalanche of shells. Its position had been
gauged with devilish nicety—shell after shell
fell just short or over each gun emplacement,
kicking great clouds of black smoke and
earth and débris into the air. It looked as
though every man must be blown to atoms
as we watched their diminutive forms,
smudged in the smoke, drop and run and
drop amidst the inferno of this annihilating
clamour. I gazed in fear and awe as spurt
and crash followed with breathless rapidity,
and one man after another darted away to
safety. For twenty minutes the shelling
continued and when it ceased it seemed that
nothing short of a miracle had actually
spared not only every man but every gun.
Not a man and not a gun hit, while closely
circling the battery position the earth was
pockmarked with huge craters.

After that it was with genuine pleasure
that we watched a fight in the air and saw the
German plane shot down. I marvelled at the
way it fell. Once it had veered and turned on
its side I expected to see it go hurtling to

47

earth, but it fell so straight and slowly, with one great wing pointing to the ground, that it seemed actually suspended by a gradually lengthening, invisible cable. One seemed to have been watching it for an age before it finally reached the ground. It fell on a dugout, burying two men, who had to be shovelled out. The pilot had been shot through the head. As it landed, souvenir hunters rushed up to it from all directions, and, being in the open and in full view of the Germans, were promptly shot at.

5

From time to time the mess needed replenishment and I was given an opportunity to ride, if but for a few hours, away from it all. These were rare and joyous occasions when one tasted the sweetness of complete solitude. In war one is seldom alone.

Into Dickebush I rode, with its main street on one side of which all the houses had been hit and deserted, while the other side

48

remained untouched and inhabited. The ingenious sign " Don't go further and get shelled. Do your shopping in Dickebush " (put up no doubt when Ypres was still inhabited, and now that Dickebush is the furthermost inhabited village, quite out of date) could not fail, however, to appeal to me.

As the short day drew to a close I turned about. The moon was up, faintly lighting the way. We ambled on, my mind astray with thoughts very far from my immediate surroundings (on Dorothy perhaps) when the first frightening screech of a shell tore over our heads and burst behind us. I was congratulating myself on a narrow escape when the second shell screamed over. And then we burst into a gallop with shell after shell spinning over our heads and " crumping " behind us. It was like a cavalry charge and I was thrilled—although which was the more dangerous, the shells or the wild gallop over broken and treacherous country, I do not know.

But my days in the salient were drawing to a close and I was actually sitting in the

Observation Post doing F.O.O. when I read in the Gazette of my transfer to the Grenadier Guards.*

That night I said good-bye to my brother officers mounted my charger and trotted out of the Ypres salient. It was a night that, as long as I live, will live with me. The salient, which was the smouldering volcano of the British front, had become unusually quiet. In the distance the muffled sound of gunfire had died away leaving one of those strange, sudden, inexplicable and complete silences that occurred at rare intervals at the front—a silence which the night wore like a mask.

The slip of a moon lit everything to the degree of a single candle in a curtained room.

It was odd to be suddenly released like this. I felt as a dog might, let out on a long leash that would eventually be drawn in—drawn in the tighter.

---

* Hugo Rumbold did much to effect my transfer. Wounded in a brewery in 1914 and, carried back on a stretcher, he passed a brother officer. "Hit, Hugo?" "Hit," replied Hugo, "by a piece of sweet shell of old brewery!"

Chapter IV

I

LONDON! Not with the uncertain footing
of a week's leave, but London for several
months, with time to take on anew the habit
of pre-war existence.

I reported to the Lieutenant Colonel, who
received me with that gracious courtesy
peculiar to people in high places. He
made this temporary second-lieutenant—this
" guest " of the Grenadiers—feel a positive
addition to the Regiment!

Then Chelsea Barracks. Could any two
people have been kinder than the Commanding Officer and the Adjutant? Little
enough said, but that with a personal note.
And this is a Regiment renowned for its
emphasis on the strictest discipline! Whose
success is based on it. Yes, but discipline
is not confused, and the discipline that
exists to a point of the highest efficiency
on parade yields to condescension off duty.

Two things are thus realised, high soldierly qualities combined with individuality. Along with discipline, personality is developed, and that means leadership.

The ante-room was thronged with officers, some resuming duty after sick-leave and wounds, but mostly young officers—by young I mean newly-joined, for they included boys from Sandhurst and public schools, more seasoned men in their twenties, transfers from other regiments and not a few " elderly gentlemen " between forty and fifty.

Before being ready for the front you are first " on the square," a part of your training on which the most emphasis is laid. It is while on the square that the conscious fact of being a Guardsman is inculcated, through the simple process of being made to execute drill movements as nearly like a machine as possible. Endlessly turning to the left and to the right, but done with a snap and precision. . . . " Don't flap your arms about like angels' wings ! " But there is no desire to laugh at the drill sergeant's cutting

comments. I have forgotten his name, but a
smarter man than this non-commissioned
officer doesn't exist. " That man ! Don't
think about what you did last night ! " . . .
" Put more dash into it, put more devil
be'ind it," and indeed we attempted to,
officers and men commingled, and I little
realised that each muscular jerk was making
me just that much more a Guardsman and a
soldier.

Outside of soldiering I lived without plan
but with activity. I saw little of Dorothy.
I went a good deal to Ciro's. I saw a lot
of a girl named Irene West. She had red
hair, a pale face and a pert and pretty nose.
She was like a petal—she was somehow less
than a flower. Everything turned up and
at the same angle—her nose, her upper lip
and chin. She even had a way of looking
at the top of your head when you talked
to her. It always made me think my hair
was mussed. She never smiled at any joke,
but she laughed a lot. She was gay within.
She laughed and danced and drank a great
deal. She made life worth while—that

particular life which belonged to that particular time.

I thought about her on parade. As I turned about and to the left and to the right, facing the barracks, the quartermaster's stores or the officers' ante-room, I pictured the evening that lay ahead.

I wonder what happened to girls like Irene after the war. They disappeared as completely as the men who were killed. They were a soldier's true companions. The excitement, the adventure, the risk of living involved them also. There existed a ready-made sympathy between the two.

I didn't really feature Irene, though we dined together constantly. Others joined us. I liked wandering from table to table talking to men I knew and meeting other women. In the end I would frequently discover that Irene had left with another man. In the end I often took someone else home. It was a haphazard existence. The point was to take someone home.

When I did call on Dorothy, she made me feel as tired as perhaps I actually was. When she sang " They are not long, the weeping and the laughter," I nearly fell asleep.

The next morning I remained in bed. I wanted to get up but couldn't, or I could have got up but did not want to, it was difficult to make out which. Well, I was missing parade. I had to do something about that. I called in Dr. Milligan. When he arrived I said, " I must have a certificate to say I am ill. I'm missing parade."

He put a thermometer in my mouth and felt my pulse. I opened my mouth.

" Don't talk," he said. " How long have you been feeling this way ? "

I started to tell him. " Don't talk," he said.

He took the thermometer out and studied it. " You *are* ill," he announced.

" What is my temperature ? "

He would not tell me. Now that my condition had been definitely established between us, I felt ill. That was a comfort.

" Sit up ! "

He lifted my pyjama jacket and beat a tattoo on my back. His fingers felt cold.

He pressed his ear against my back. His beard scratched. " Say ninety-nine."

" Ninety-nine."

" Take a deep breath."

" That hurts."

" Where ? "

" Here."

" Can you send out for this medicine ? "

He took out a fountain pen and began to write hieroglyphics on a small pad with his name on the top.

" Of course."

" Stay in bed, drink a lot of water. I'll come and see you this evening."

" Isn't this a nuisance ? " but I felt relieved.

" Just a touch of 'flu."

When he had left I wanted to ring up Irene, but the effort required seemed too great. Then I thought I would telephone Dorothy, but at that moment I discovered a crack in the ceiling and following its river-like course took my mind off Dorothy. After the medicine had arrived and I had taken a dose I felt drowsy and fell asleep.

The next morning I felt worse. . . .

While I was convalescing Irene came to see me. She fidgeted on the edge of a chair. She smoked innumerable cigarettes. Outside of Ciro's we seemed to have nothing in common. The idea of Ciro's was not at the moment attractive.

Irene did not stay long, nor did she come again.

One afternoon Dorothy came to see me. She looked at home on a small straight chair. She wore a tailor-made suit of green cloth with a fur collar. She was lovely and full of health. I was glad to see her.

She held a roll of music in her gloved hand. When I asked her what the songs were, she came and sat on the edge of my bed. There was a coolness about her dress. It was a clear cold winter's day and the slanting sunshine brightened the houses opposite, and struck the windows in such a way that the rooms appeared lighted within.

" Reynaldo Hahn," she said.

I opened the sheet of music and started to read the words out loud.

" ' Voici des fruits, des fleurs, des feuilles
et des branches ' . . . My favourite poem
by Verlaine is ' Je fais souvent ce rêve
étrange et pénétrant d'une femme inconnue
que j'aime et qui m'aime.' " I ran the two
lines together.

" Mine," she replied, " is," and she sang :

" Voici des fruits, des fleurs, des feuilles et
des branches,
Et puis voici mon cœur qui ne bat que
pour vous."

When she had finished I said, " I feel as
though the war were an illusion. I don't
mean I feel there isn't going to be a war, I
feel there is going to be one all right, but as
though it had been put off. I just feel as
though there wasn't a war now."

Dorothy rose.

" Everything always comes back to the
war."

" I think I can get sick leave in the south of
France. I wish you were going to be there."

She looked at me. " Perhaps I could
manage it. I might be able to stay with

Elsie Lateley. She has a villa at Cannes. I'm not sure she isn't there now."

She gazed questioningly at me. She seemed not to be thinking of Elsie Lateley and the villa. I don't quite know what she was thinking about.

When I had obtained a month's leave on the Riviera Dorothy told me she could not get away. . . .

The train moved behind mountains that seemed a rampart thrown up to shut out the war. The pine, the palm and the olive tree, the asphodel and the white convolvulus carried the spirit still further afield. Peace reigned. Blue day followed close upon blue day, and I remembered the war as an unpleasant and exacting engagement made some time ahead.

2

It was in September that I received my bit of paper—" You should hold yourself in readiness to proceed overseas at an early date." On the 15th the Division had gone into battle and the 3rd Battalion had had fifteen out of seventeen officers hit.

That night I dined with my father. We said little—there was too much to say. The meal went deftly to a finish, while I hugged to myself the luxury of dining in that house. I took in the warm red brocade curtains, the pictures (three Van Goyens and a fine Stubbs) and the Queen Anne candle sticks, in a lingering and individual gaze.

I left my father standing on the front doorstep, a protective expanse to his white shirt front that would haunt me in the days to come.

With no rendezvous and yet no desire to go to bed I walked to Ciro's. As I stood in the doorway I gazed upon a scene to which, by the minute's spiritual transition, I had ceased to belong. These people, these lights, the smoke, the yellow plush banquettes, the music, the motion, the synthetic smell of perfume and powder and flesh and food, all served but to accentuate my isolation. An imminent experience had thrown the present out of focus. I was going out to be shot,

shot at. I looked on with an inward eye.

Turning about I walked to my flat in Charles Street. A vague night had turned into a drizzle. Along Piccadilly each hooded lamp threw out a radiance like a fairy parasol, and the searchlights stabbed shortsightedly at the night.

My footsteps struck muffled solitary notes.

After I had entered I was reluctant to go to bed. Sleep meant waking up and another day gone. Life stretched away in a down grade of moments of suspense and danger and discomfort and boredom, to the possible gulf of ultimate annihilation.

3

We left Waterloo Station on the 21st of September, eight of us, embarked at Southampton and reaching Le Havre the next morning proceeded to the Guards Divisional Base Depot at Harfleur. Harfleur! Five hundred years ago Henry V had taken it from the French. We still seemed to have it! Here we were billeted in huts, two officers per hut. Paths with trim herbaceous borders gave to the camp, for its transient inhabitants, a final touch of home before the train that took one up to the front had jerked slowly out of the station at Le Havre. Around the table in the officers' mess one pondered over the lists of casualties that, occurring on the 15th, had begun to appear in the " Roll of Honour." But not for long. We were needed to fill the gaps and remained at Harfleur scarcely more than a day or two before we received orders to join the Division.

The train left Le Havre in the evening. Sitting up in day-coaches, smoking, or gazing for the " umpteenth " time at that most familiar of war notices " Taisez-vous ! Méfiez-vous ! les oreilles ennemies vous écoutent," or falling into a sleep that was forever being interrupted by the continual halting of the train, we reached Rouen in the morning. Some eight to ten hours to complete a journey that once took an hour.

We had hoped to make a decent stop there, but soon we were on our way again, bound for Amiens. We detrained near Albert where I saw for the first time the statue of the Virgin Mary hanging at an angle of over fifty degrees from the church steeple. The common superstition was that its fall would signalise the end of the war. (It did fall in 1918 under a heavy German bombardment and the war ended that year.)

The Guards Division had attacked that morning, September 25th, and we were told had captured all its objectives. The 3rd Battalion was in reserve. I joined it while the men were having their suppers, preparatory to moving off.

That night we bivouacked in Trônes Wood. It remained a wood only in name. It had been swept with shell-fire until there was not a tree that had not been stripped of leaf and branch. Trees uprooted stretched across one's path. Everywhere was the litter and débris of battle. An overturned six-inch German howitzer, an unexploded twelve-inch British shell, gun limbers, wheels, helmets, cartridges, big dugouts caved in by direct hits, bits of dead men and scattered clothing ripped from bodies by the back blast of big shells, and a few hurried shallow graves. Near the wood a village once existed. It had so literally vanished that not the dust of a single brick could be detected.

So crowded with troops was the valley below that the campfires and lights gave the illusion of a big city. These were the days before intensive bombing.

I passed the night in a shell hole, and the naked trees of Trônes Wood could not screen the stars overhead from my wakeful eyes. The guns were restless after the battle and the bark of the 18-pounders and the boom of the heavies continued throughout the night.

Burial parties were sent out in the morning and I was glad not to have been included in this grim task. The corpses to be interred were ten days old—British and German. Each body's identity had if possible to be established before burial. The stench and appearance of the dead was such that the young soldiers were sick. N.C.O.'s and old soldiers had to do most of the work. As the labour proceeded the men were shelled, although many of the bodies they buried were German.*

We remained another night in Trônes Wood and I slept better in a newly built dugout with a platoon stretcher for a bed. The third night the Battalion moved up, taking over a forward bit of trench won on the 25th. The Germans had retired to high ground about a thousand yards away. We were occasionally shelled and a man was killed on the side of the road across from the officers' dugout.

Digging a new trench in front we lost our sergeant-major, whose arm was almost blown off. He refused to be helped on the stretcher but put himself on it. He was very popular and the men were saddened.

After four days we were relieved. I took my clothes off for the first time in seven days.

4

The whole Division was in rest—a rest

*N.B.—This is incorrect. I have since heard from a member of the party, Private E. Moss, that on perceiving the nature of the work being undertaken, the Germans ceased firing.

only from fighting, for drills, parade and training went on with greater intensity than existed in Chelsea Barracks. Recruits that had filled the gaps left by the battle on September 15th had to be absorbed into the Battalion, and the Battalion itself had to continue a smoothly functioning and disciplined unit. For the accomplishment of this end there could be no momentary let up. I honestly believe that our Commanding Officer looked upon trench duty as a period of idleness to' be drastically remedied immediately the Battalion was behind the lines. To see that the Battalion kept fit games too were organised, and galloping after a hare in the short autumn afternoons was compulsory for all officers.

The officers of my Company (No. 1) were billeted in a small Louis XIV château. It was at one time tenanted by an aristocrat guillotined during the Revolution.

While on short leave in Amiens I heard about Dill Star. He wanted to go into the Flying Corps, but thought it would take too long to get to the front. Walter Oakman,

66

who had joined the Coldstream, persuaded him to transfer into that Regiment.

Dill went to France about September 1st, and was killed on the 15th of that month.

" You knew him ? " asked the young officer in the Coldstream with whom I was having a drink.

" Yes."

" He went over in fine style . . ."

And then I thought of the story told me once about Dill.   Whenever he had had a bit too much drink in his club at Harvard he could be found sitting in front of a certain picture.   It was an old coloured print and represented a charge by a regiment in the Brigade of Guards.

Meanwhile the clockwork passage of time continued.   Each day was a matter of routine marred or made by the weather.   I felt the shortening of the days and the growing cold with real concern, and when a heavy rain, followed by a frost, brought down in showers the leaves from the trees, I looked on with sorrow and dismay.   It was the unequivocal sign of approaching winter and that meant the worst fight of all—mud and wet and cold—six months of it.

Occasionally I went for a gallop alone while

" . . . my soul
Smoothed itself out a long-cramped scroll
Freshening and fluttering in the wind."

The casualties of the Somme, the failure of the Somme—like any set-back after a real test—had made the war an endless affair. One knew it to be endless and in accepting this as a fact, what chance had one of getting through? No answer. I sought, like so many others, the refuge and strength of poetry. The poetry one wrote was an endeavour to realise a sense of continuity, and a compromise with death.

But I was not to die that winter! A cold on my intestines, an intermittent fever, and I was admitted to hospital at Amiens. The hospital was near the station and one night while being bombed I felt the situation of being in bed was not the proper one.

I was evacuated to England. I saw

Dorothy once or twice. But something had rubbed her from my conscious mind. Mrs. Oliver and the Bentinck remained unchanged though less frequented.

Two days before I was due to go " out " a party took place at the Four Hundred Club (now the Embassy).

As I approached my hostess I noticed a girl, sitting next to her, so lovely that I continued to gaze at her while addressing my hostess. The hint was so obvious that I was introduced at once. I did not catch her name, so I will call her Susan. I cannot describe her, but if I *could* have done it, and had been told to invent a woman, she would have been like Susan. From that extravagant statement you may imagine the enchantment I felt.

She " made " my evening. I danced with no one else—which was rather hard on her. So absorbed did I become that I was only vaguely aware of a young man who occasionally hovered tentatively near us. When we were not dancing we talked. There were not many people ; an isolated table was not difficult to find and our interest in each other kept everyone else away.

I don't remember how we got on the subject of Americans. She had not taken me for one.

" I think American women are attractive but not the men," which was a joke on me although I did not tell her so.

It seemed natural instead to tell her extraordinary things such as, " All my life I have had my dreams and now my dreams become you, like a precious, spiritual dress." It seemed right for her to listen without laughing. That word " spiritual " was a good one. It lent solemnity and sincerity to the occasion.

" Don't you hate that war ? "

" Hate it !   Can you ask that about a war that is going to take me from you in two days."

" Are you going out as soon as that ? "

War is the more terrible for the fascinating situations it can create.   There is a charm in leave-taking to-day, should the journey's end be Paris, Palm Beach or Timbuctoo.   But then !   With the doubt as to whether one would return ever present to torment and to stimulate any sex attraction.

It was five in the morning although one would not have suspected it in this window-less room still artificially bright.

" Can I take you home ? "

" I have a husband here."

" Good God ! Where is he ? I haven't seen him."

But someone was approaching.

" Here he is."

She introduced us. He was a gay, hap-hazard youth, with the soft face of a little boy.

He turned to Susan. " Do you want to go home ? "

" I think it's time."

Whereupon he wandered off, a proceeding which I learned later was characteristic.

" I'll see you to-morrow."

" Do you think we should ? "

" I certainly do."

" Ring me up—about noon."

To go from the stuffy room into the street was to find the air turned to crystal. Lon-don, quiet enough those days, stood about me deathly still but solid and protective.

71

Chapter V

I

THE transport ship from Southampton was packed with troops. To walk the deck would have meant stepping on their recumbent forms.

Le Havre! Harfleur! The swing of the pendulum. Almost without emotion, in the repetition of war experience, one landed again. Le Havre, 1914, 1915, 1916, and now 1917. I moved about its gloomy and sodden streets, seeking that everlasting reiteration of last minute sensations which was the exclusive right of the fighting soldier, and finding no echo to my slightly immoderate laughter in the unhappy faces of its civilian population.

Tortoni every night, and a good bottle of vintage wine, which in the end but served to buoy our spirits for a long return journey to the camp at Harfleur.

The Commanding Officer and Adjutant

remained the same. Did they think, I wonder, of the hundreds of dead officers for whom they had acted as official hosts? (By the end of the war the five regiments of Foot Guards had had more than five hundred officers killed.) Did they finally shudder at the thought of " speeding glum heroes up the line to death " ?

After a few days about eight officers received orders to join the Entrenching Battalion (the " Diggers " as it was called).

I shall always remember these journeys to the front as conducted with a certain tact, quite unintentional, as the train slowly nosed its way along, with innumerable halts to allow one a still view of the peaceful countryside.

On this occasion the weather was so fine as to permit the men to bask in the sun on the roofs of their railway trucks during the train's meticulous progress. It was a dangerous thing to do, for sometimes a man was hit by some overhanging obstacle or even fell off, but, although contrary to regulations, it was difficult to stop them.

Before leaving Le Havre a party of private soldiers broke into some barrels of rum in a train next to our own. By the time we reached Amiens a man had died and several more were in a critical condition, while the rest of the party on being turned out made a pitiable pretence of standing to attention. The O.C. Train turned up to inspect a group that the pencil of Daumier or Orpen could have made tragically grotesque. Stretchers removed casualties as real as those of battle, while French railway officials looked on in wonder, and I thought of the mighty thirst that comes on men bound for rather more than probable doom.

The days in the " Diggers " linger in my affections. The weather was continuously fine though sizzling, but our boiling marches to points where small trench systems were dug or strengthened and roads mended, were compensated for by the luxury of hot baths in rubber tubs and the remainder of long summer afternoons spent writing precious letters, with an eye to getting immediate answers, or over books packed in London for just such occasions.

At night we were a merry company. A composite and shifting battalion of officers of all five regiments of the Brigade of Guards, there was no seniority and no authority but that of the Commanding Officer, Major Ellice. He was the perfect type of Foot Guards officer, with that sublime ability to exercise authority and inspire obedience by day, combined with a supreme capacity to unbend when off duty. He made himself one of us and joined in our jokes and laughter and lingered with us, listening to our songs. He was a child at heart and so could look upon us as children, whose time for playing was short, and the death of his only son had sweetened, not embittered him.

So passed these last valuable days of comparative ease and safety. Once for an hour only we were shelled, with a single casualty—one man shell-shocked. (Shell-shock is gauged by the fact that a man's pulse and temperature go up, while he is temporarily paralysed and unable to speak.)

Once I visited a graveyard, to ruminate on
the fact that French and German and British
lay peacefully together while I listened to the
angry rumble of distant battle. And when
we heard the Guards Division had " gone
into it," we knew (so instinctive is the
thought of self) that our time for leaving the
" Diggers " was at hand. I thought of
that as I read in my London *Times* of
August 1st, " The way the Guards went
through was as fine a sight as has ever been
seen on any battlefield." News nicely
seasoned for home consumption ; and did
he see them go over with the naked eye?
I saw nothing a few weeks hence of the
battle on whose immediate left we stood.
But it was true that the Division had penetrated deep to all its objectives in spite of
the German " pill-boxes ". It was said these
small concrete forts but served to imprison
their garrisons in the end, for the protection
from shell-fire that the occupants enjoyed
they were loath to give up.

But before I left the " Diggers " I got
one short leave in Amiens. From Roisel (a

village in that part of the country evacuated
by the enemy in the spring of 1917) to
Amiens took one through the blasted Somme
battlefield. Fields once ploughed with shells
had gained a veneer of ancient respectability
in an uneven covering of green. Trees not
quite dead had produced odd tufts and
growths, clothing awkwardly their former
utter nakedness. Through this shattered
area, a battlefield which, with the war still
on, was already out of date, civilisation was
stretching its fingers, and roads and railways
took one along an area that was once
complete desolation.

I was glad that the Germans had abandoned it so that its thousands and thousands
of dead might lie at peace.

But I forgot the Somme as we enjoyed the
brief civilian comfort of walking between
houses, and went through the ritual of a
rich dinner at the Godbert.

2

The battle north meant casualties and

casualties meant, for us, a shortening of our
sojourn with the " Diggers." Six of us
received word to join our battalions, and
we paraded for the last time under the
paternal eye of Major Ellice; six officers
and three hundred and thirty-six other ranks
to help keep to a numerical level various
units of the Division.

The Division being north of Ypres we,
at the other end of the British front, had a
long journey before us. We travelled with
the extremity of discomfort in freight cars,
and I have to-day a photograph of my five
companions, standing outside our truck, and
the memory that four of them were killed
afterwards.

During a long night we slept on our hard
bed of wood and it was a relief when the
train jerked into Abbeville and stopped long
enough for us to get out and walk to the
hotel and breakfast. News reached us of
the toll the recent battle had taken and I
for one approached the horizon line of continued and continuing battle in a mood of
deep dejection. The act of taking a train,

though under orders, had about it an element of volition which no doubt accounted for this ; certainly it disappeared and was substituted by a more mechanical attitude of mind as soon as I became again identified with the routine life of a battalion. But I left Abbeville with misgivings ; so much more fearful is premonition than actuality.

Late the next night—so slow and disjointed were these journeys, whose mileage was nevertheless absurdly small—we came to a heavy halt at Houpoutel and I spent another night en route and this time at Poperinghe—affectionately called " Pop " by the entire British Army. Although occasionally shelled and bombed, it was the last (or the first, according to which way you were headed) inhabited town. I remember it for two things—La Poupée (a restaurant), and a shop where I bought gramophone records. Next to the shop stood a ruined house, destroyed by a bomb. I mentioned this to the young girl waiting on me and she assented politely as though I had said " What a nice day." They had real courage, these women—the courage to carry on their jobs, which meant making money, while the war lasted.

The next morning I joined the Battalion, which was in rest. Not quite a year had passed. The Commanding Officer, " Bulgy " Thorne, the second-in-command, Guy Rasch, and four officers, John Craigie, Hirst, Fryer, Alec Robartes, all on the Somme when I originally joined, were still with the Battalion. The others had replaced casualties. A number, too, had come and gone during my absence.

3

Soon I got a look at the battlefield as I paraded early with a party under Major Rasch, the second-in-command. We embussed, entrained and detrained at Elverdinghe. An hour's march brought us to the canal over which the Division had crossed at the beginning of the attack. Almost at my feet was one of the narrow duckboard bridges over which the men had passed;

chipped and splintered with shell and bullet, it seemed incredible to me that any of the men had been able to reach the other side. Soon the party were busy making a plank road. We were next to a battery of 18-pounders which barked away unceasingly. The whole front was active and impending battle was in the air.

The following day a cricket match took place between our own and another battalion. The Prince of Wales made it the occasion of a visit. He remained among us for an hour. As I watched his pink and amiable face and felt his simple friendliness I understood his popularity—that rare popularity that touches the affections.

The next morning the Battalion moved up and the Division was in support to the 29th Division, who, with the 20th, attacked and took Langemark and established themselves on the "Red Line." The Battalion was now in huts at a place called De Wippe Cabaret.

The rumble of battle died away and on a clear night I realized how the area of war had deepened when I watched a German aeroplane flying over and dropping bombs. Soon the sky was interlaced with searchlights which jabbed and swept until the plane was caught in the track of one like a moth in a flame.

Battle like suppressed thunder hovered in the air, as we had a rehearsal of what we were expected to do within the next few weeks. The creeping barrage had given way to the " bounding " barrage. One line was shelled for six minutes, then the barrage lifted and went forward a hundred yards and played on the next line for six minutes. This was because the enemy had been driven out of his trench system and relied on shell holes to hold up an attack. The creeping barrage often missed these odd groups of shell holes.

4

From De Wippe Cabaret, that gloomy spot with a cheery name, we moved to Eton Camp. The Division had gone into the line and we were Battalion in reserve. From now on we were " in the war," and not a day passed without a due reminder of that fact.

It was not necessary to be in the front line trenches any longer to feel the full, fierce force of war. Long range shelling and bombing from aeroplanes were of daily occurrence, and the back areas were so " over populated " that a man being hit stood an equal chance with a fly slapped at on the wall. Our camp was bounded by a road, a railway and a decaville railway ; the former two would be marked on any map and all three would show up well on an aeroplane photograph.

Fine nights were therefore not wanted, for they brought out the enemy aeroplane, whose buzzing overhead was the certain prelude to a bomb.

We escaped not his visitation. We received it and with a vengeance, though by some miraculous chance three of the four companies were still out on " fatigues " when the five bombs pricked the surface of our small camp. Each bomb made indeed no more than a pin prick as it burst on graze with a tremendous lateral spread.

I was sleeping soundly when the first crash awakened me into dizzy reality. Twenty yards from my tent, it might as well have been in the tent, its blinding proximity, like a flashlight photograph, was so at one with the sense of contact. Another bomb followed a few seconds later with the same blazing finality that included me in its headlong destruction. I was dimly aware that the third kicked a fraction further away; the fourth followed suit, while the fifth and last struck the far corner of the camp as the engines of the aeroplane whirred to a rapid diminuendo.

I lay a minute conscious of the terror I had experienced. Perhaps it was because of the crash that the silence succeeding was so intense. Could no one have been hit?

There followed a confusion of sound—a medley of voices in pain and alarm—strangely subdued.

I slipped out of my sleeping bag and with an electric torch hurried into a clear and starlit night. Soon I pressed the catch which put out the torch as I came across the wounded, dead and dying—men of No. 1 Company who but a few minutes before

84

had been drinking hot tea after a night's "fatigue."

Sparks from the Company cooker had been seen by the aeroplane. The Company cooker had paid the penalty; had been hit and tossed twenty yards by the first bomb, while the water cart had been turned into kindling wood.

I wandered unhappily among the poor men, sick at the sight of such a nightmare of suffering; speaking a word to one or two, while others tended their wounds. I could not.

Ambulances arrived and the return journey began for twenty-seven men, many of whom would not reach home and some who did . . .

At about 4 a.m. I was awakened by a thunderstorm more terrifying because of the bombing than the bombing itself had been.

The following morning " graves " were dug in each of which an individual slept. Protection was thus procured from everything except a direct hit. The rest of our casualties, however, occurred by day. An afternoon's bombing wounded an officer and his servant but killed thirty-one horses in an adjoining artillery "wagon lines." The same afternoon a shell hit one of our bivouacs, killing and wounding its six occupants. Still again we were shelled with no casualties, although a shell pitched just over Battalion Headquarters mess.

The next day I watched an aeroplane shot down. The pilot—a minute spot against the sky—dropped out as it began to fall. The plane itself burst into flames, and being a long way off looked no bigger than the flare of a match tossed away by a cigarette smoker.

From time to time the air was filled with the rumble of artillery—so intense and continuous that there was no second of cessation, and I thought of Loos as an old-fashioned battle, so tremendously had artillery fire increased. It was well named—drum fire —its volume was the roll of millions of mighty drums.

Sometimes the firing went on all night as some small attack was anticipated. Then the quiet of the morning following would seem Sabbath-like in its stillness. We ourselves

were finally included in one of these pro-
jected advances—we and the 1st Coldstream.
The idea was to establish a line well over the
Broembeek (a narrow sluggish stream) so as
to give the next attacking troops a jumping-
off place that would eliminate crossing the
river.

The attack was cancelled although its plan
lasted sufficiently long for my sniper, Sergeant Wonnacott, and me to go on two long
reconnaissance trips to the front line.

Our first journey took place on a night
moonless and misty. After crossing the canal
we went gingerly along the duckboards that
followed like a trail the high ground through
a multitude of shell holes. Everywhere the
earth had been churned up as though by
some colossal and crazy plough. It was six
miles to the front line and back and we returned to the measure of a great deal of " uncertain " shelling ; uncertain in the sense of
no particular point being shelled so much
as the whole area searched.

Our second journey occurred by day. Our
walk took us the entire depth of the advance

begun July 31st. But an afternoon's stroll
to penetrate the extent of ground which it
had cost so many lives to win. We passed
Elverdinghe, through Boesinghe, and again
along Hunter Street to Military Road, while
my eye took in by day this solidified sea of
mud. The enemy were not shelling, but I
found myself in the lee of our own guns
as they began a bombardment on a large
scale. Turning about, I got an idea of the
power and concentration of the British
artillery, as I watched one flash after another
the length of an interminable line that suggested gun literally wheel to wheel with gun.
The din was terrific and sounded as though
the earth were cracking up like an egg of
super-gigantic proportions tapped by a Gar-
gantuan spoon. A hundred and fifty yards
away a flash and cloud of smoke indicated a
" premature." A bit of metal, singing
through the air, landed at our feet. On
examination it proved to be a part of the
barrel of a gun, six inches in diameter. We
looked up to see a man being carried away.

We pushed on past German pill-boxes,

square, concreted, squat buildings into which
the German infantry had crowded while the
mighty British artillery preparation had
pounded around them; past the débris of
battle, heavy German armour breast plates
used by shock troops, smashed guns, an
overturned railway truck, a horse long dead,
still in its trappings of German make, and
stripped and naked trees, until we reached
Battalion Headquarters. Here we stopped
for a cup of tea.

After this refreshment I left its candle-lit
interior and gazed anew upon a bleak and
flattened landscape. Cautiously we approached the ruin known as Martin's Mill,
and from it through field glasses I made
out certain prominences and densities and
tried to determine what they were. Again
we moved forward around shell holes up
to a pill-box near Cannes Farm which was
on the left of the support company's position, and from here we picked out, with
the imagination as well as with the naked
eye, pill-boxes and organized shell holes and
belts of barbed wire. Satisfied with this

strange inspection we turned about ; I, rather scared, now that no object existed but to get safely back to the Battalion. Without incident we reached Military Road and had gone some way along it when a shell screamed closely overhead. On our way up to the line Wonnacott had made an astounding observation. " That man bobs," he had said. " Bobs ? " I had repeated, not understanding, and visualising a dip to royalty. " Yes, bobs," insisted Wonnacott. " That man ducks under shellfire." I gazed at Wonnacott. He wore the D.C.M. and a Russian Order, both won for gallantry in the field. A brave man, Wonnacott, I thought. Now with this first shell I had felt the instinctive slump—" bobbed " indeed had I, while Wonnacott shamed me by remaining upright, unmoved. My courage was being put to the test. " Oh, well," I think, " just a stray shell." But I was quickly undeceived and we were walking straight for the spot on which they were falling. I paused. Wonnacott stopped, impassive. Another shell,which fell somewhat short of the others. They

were " searching " the road. " I think," said
I tentatively, " we'd better cut across country
until we strike Clarges Street," and I acted
quickly on my words, slithering with the
extreme of agility into a shell hole as another
shell arrived whose detonation was closer
still. Wonnacott had nought to do but obey
an officer. From crater to crater we climbed
quickly, while shell after shell crashed on to
Military Road. Finally we reached Clarges
Street. Along its duckboards we wound
our way ; stopping to look back in the fading
light, the horizon was lit by a medley of
big and little flashes—an enemy ammunition
dump exploded by a British shell.

The next evening John Craigie, Frank
Eaton and I got short leave to " Pop." We
dined at La Poupée. We drank Paul
Ruinart 1900 in that quantity which suggested a desire not so much to quench the
thirst as to drown the body and the soul.

5

After eight days in Eton Camp, the

Battalion moved to Rugby Camp and became
" Battalion in support." The camp was nicely
situated next to a battery of heavies, who
fired all day and on whom the Boche retali-
ated at night, so that Rugby Camp came in
for its share of shelling.   There were French
next to us, in a state of fury at the stupidity
of guns being near an infantry camp. They,
too, got some of the shells intended for the
battery. The shell used by the Germans
was from a six-inch armour-piercing naval
gun which made an enormous hole, but had
no spread, so unless you were unlucky
enough to have had it land on top of you,
you were comparatively safe.

It was a grey impersonal day when we
" took over "—a relief, because bad visibility
brought less shelling. Until night all remained quiet. The war turned over on its
side and went to sleep. During the night it
rained—but later on the weather proved no
hindrance, and we were shelled at intervals,
although without casualties, until early
morning. My cot had been lowered into
a deep grave, in spite of which security I

had the sensation of being elevated to the level of the earth's surface with each burst of a shell.

This explosion of a shell in the dead of night, bringing the unconscious mind rudely back into a moment's breathless, vivid consciousness, was a most terrifying thing. I used to think I was a part of the war, but later I knew the war had forever become a part of me.

The morning broke chill and grey, which was an ill wind that blew some good, for shelling stopped for a space, while I became chiefly concerned over having lost a luck charm—a particular kind of small stone in the shape of a cross, said to be always found that way, sent me from America. I looked for it feverishly while I thought of poor Baker of the First Battalion. On "Paris leave" a lady had approached me, and, introducing herself as the wife of Captain Baker, asked me to take a letter to him. "I am worried because he has lost a luck charm I had given him," she reflected. "Of course," she added, "I know it's all right." That

was about the 12th of July. He was killed
the end of the month.

I found my own luck charm before taking
a third trip to the front line—uneventful
except for a salvo of four shells which
whistled close overhead and banged down at
a point we had been some minutes before.
I thought of my cross and moved with a
quicker step.

On getting back to camp the weather
cleared and the evening was so beautiful, so
meant to be peaceful in its beauty, that even
the guns took the hint and were silent for
a time.

Not for long, however, and tumult
reigned throughout a night during which
various messages led the higher command to
expect something and we stood to at 6 a.m.
But nothing happened.

That night we were lightly shelled during
dinner. It was case of eating and running !
Before retiring I looked into a sky that held
every star. Although there was much shelling during the night, I slept like a man
grown accustomed to living in a draughty

house of banging doors.

It was at this time we heard a grand story about the Irish Guards who were in the line. The Germans launched a well-organized attack with troops in armour breast plates on some advanced posts or occupied shell holes—thrown out over the enemy side of the Broembeek River. One section under a sergeant held out in a "strong point" for two days and two nights. They had only the water in their water bottles, and for food only their emergency rations. The fourth night they beat off a strong attack and, led by the sergeant, carried their wounded and fought their way through the enemy, crossed the Broembeek and reported to their Commanding Officer. The Commanding Officer heard the story from the sergeant but noticed that the men were in a half-starved condition. The sergeant explained that they hadn't had anything to eat for two days.

"What about your emergency rations?"

"Oh," replied the sergeant, "we kept

those for an emergency ! "

One officer, during the preliminary bombardment, had two " duds " land in his
shell hole, one of which killed his orderly.
The battalion suffered some 106 casualties.

*   *

*

Chapter VI

I

IT was dusk. The men were falling in. The evening was quiet. The night sinister and sombre. The men looked ominous, set and serious—a visual translation of my own sensations. I listened to the simple words of command and read in them an added meaning and a new significance.

" Slope arms—move to the right in fours —form fours—right—by the left, quick march." We stepped out while some gunners watched with admiration those slightly supermen—the Guards.

"We're givin' 'em socks to-night," said one.

We reached White Hope Corner, and then that inevitable halt. I watched the huddled remnant of Boesinghe Wood tremble to an occasional flare. The men talked in whispers or were silent. Silent mostly. No smoking allowed, of course, just when one most needed a cigarette.

97

After what seemed an interminable time we moved on, halted again, moved, halted— it tried one's nerves. At last we struck the duckboards—Clarges Street, with enemy shells falling well to our right.

"Good old Military Road again," I thought. "That old road is certainly living up to its name."

Now and then we were threatened as a shell dropped close, and once I tripped and fell flat on my face.

Can anything be slower than these night reliefs, whose speed is controlled by the darkness, the difficult way and the responsibility each man had for the man behind him?

We approached Cannes Farm while it was a target for enemy shelling and a party of Scots Guards scattered from it and among us, and to avoid a mix up we proceeded straight into the zone of fire.

The men were seen into shallow slits where they were packed as tight as sardines in boxes. No trench system there; dig down until you strike water, which was at a depth of about three feet, and get what protection you could.

The officers were better off in a tiny pill-box, a new entrance to which had been made by a British shell, so narrow that to get inside you had to take off all your equipment.

After a time I made a tour of our lines. We were " Company in support." Two companies were in the front line and the fourth in reserve. The night was dark as pitch and threatened rain. I tripped on some loose strands of barbed wire and cut my hand. Although there was a certain amount of shelling, we had so far escaped casualties.

The night passed. The following day the Company received orders to extend to the right. Company Headquarters was to move to the extreme right of the Company in a block-house between the road and the railway, and the Company would thus occupy a wider frontage. We were informed that the division on our right flank was to attack on the 20th, and as the British bombard-ment would begin about three in the morning, it behoved the Company to be dug in before that time. At nightfall three platoons " felt " their right and dug, while Company Headquarters took an unusual time to travel its few hundred yards in a dark night, over a country with no remaining landmarks but the block-house itself that we had to reach. An occasional flare faintly radiated a morass of shell craters, as we slipped and floundered over its wet, uneven surface. The officers' servants actually took from 7 to 2.30 to cover the distance. Three days' rations were distributed and at 1 a.m. I went along the line and found everyone dug in. I returned, feeling the quiet ominously, because of the noise that would soon begin. We waited, with more frequent looks at our watches than the passage of time required. An uncanny stillness reigned.

2

Our new Company Headquarters was an exceptionally large and powerfully built pill-box. A hole in its side made by a direct hit

from a British heavy enabled one to measure
the thickness of its walls—three to four feet in
depth.　The floor was uneven with fallen
débris and masonry and the air was foul.
Eaton was writing a requisition of some sort
in his notebook.　The pay-sergeant had
arrived about rations. The room was crowded
with runners, orderlies, servants, stretcher
bearers and the sergeant-major.　I observed
them with a kind of expectancy as the first
British shell, like tearing silk, came whizzing
overhead.　In a breathless second every gun
in the crowded British area had opened fire.
It was a signal for which the Boche was waiting, as shell after shell came crashing around
us.　Our pill-box, solid though it was, trem-
bled like a frightened man when a shell
landed with more than ordinary proximity.
On and on it went, this demoniac uproar that
sundered air particles and spun them into
everlasting reverberations.　The earth was
splitting up—splitting its sides—what a joke !
Blinding flash after flash lighted up the faces
of the men, too appalled to be scared.　The
angry clang of metal struck against the

exterior of the pill-box or whined through
the air in an agony of search, while we waited
for the shell that would send us to eternity.
But hell itself can get out of breath, and
there came a gradual let up.

Dawn showed no paler than the faces of
officers and men.

With the morning light we found a German corpse in our pill-box half buried in clay
and mortar. Hence the terrible stench. With
great difficulty he was dug up, and given as
decent a burial outside as haste permitted.

Eaton and I went along slits that had now
a welter of fresh shell holes around them,
while the company itself had miraculously
escaped. The men gazed at us with white
expressionless faces and I thought how like
death a face became when utterly wearied out.

About four in the afternoon our artillery
was hard at it again. Guns—guns—guns—
the whole world was made up of them.
Thunder cut up for cannon mouths, thunder
at last free of the heavens and running wild
over the earth—lightning, sneaking under
the earth and kicking it full of holes. All

night the earth shook and the air vibrated with the noise of guns and shells—English guns and German shells in an endless terrifying din of reiteration.

A direct hit on our pill-box rocked the place like a boat caught in the trough of the sea.

There was no sleep for anyone. Through the long hours the nightmare persisted until at 5.40 a.m. the division on our right went over the top to the tune of the most mighty cannonade conceivable, and my life reached a peak of auricular experience. It was at last the whole world crashing about our ears. Gunfire had, at a moment, leaped into an intensity no human being could have realised without hearing. A veritable crescendo of sounds, so continuous as to merge and blend into a single annihilating roar, the roar of a train in a tunnel magnified a millionfold; only the rattle of the machine gun barrage, like clocks gone mad, ticking out the end of time in a final breathless reckoning, rose above it, while the accelerating blasts of enemy shells added weight to the crowning catastrophe. One imagined the very air ripped and torn by the flight of numberless shells, the very sky to have become a tattered blue garment.

I went to the entrance of our pill-box to see what I could of the battle and never was spectator so thrilled, so awed. Beyond the enemy lines, behind the high dust of battle, colour stole shamefacedly into the sky; the rising sun appeared, a blurred and murky mass. The light of another day crept chill and faint over a scene too desolate for further destruction. Great clouds of smoke and dirt spouted into the air and drifted like a dirty morning mist along the horizon line. Showers of sparks, made by incendiary shells, burst like monster fire crackers, while enemy rockets, signalling that the attack had begun, shot into the sky, breaking from red into green lights, like dragons' eyes changing colour. Of troops I could see little. Specks too much the tone of the earth over which they were moving. For me the battle continued, a hurling and crashing of huge projectiles . . .

After a little, orderlies appeared coming back at the double, while soon after zero the sky was dotted with our contact aeroplanes. One came down in our lines.

The very day, made restless by its predecessors, gave us no peace, and shelling kept up, heavy as ever, while a tour of the Company's front revealed the fact that it had escaped the terrible bombardment of the night with one man killed and a man " buried."

All day the firing went on, until 6 p.m., when it turned again from scattered knocks into the prolonged, concerted bang of gun fire—attack or counter-attack? But one heard nothing and knew nothing except what was happening to one's own Company —and not always much of that.

3

In the evening I was on trench duty. I sat with my back up against the end of the platoon slit, gazing at the blurred figure of the sentry or into a sky set with stars, hard and brilliant as precious stones. Fleecy clouds, like gauze, rubbed them to a brighter lustre. I spoke in an undertone to the sentry. I felt friendliness for him. I did not know his name—one of a hundred and fifty men—how long would he last? For the matter of that how long would I? But we were one now. Reacting identically. One through a common danger. Victims of the same caprice of fate. He watched out for me and if he gave the alarm, would I not act at once for him?

I smoked a cigarette. How life balanced! Here was a hundred per cent danger and discomfort, but here too was a hundred per cent pleasure out of a cigarette. Each puff was a brief, sweet intoxicant. A suggestion of past joys, drawn deep and fragrantly into the lungs and blown out into the crystal air.

Falling into a slight doze, I woke, feeling chilled. The darkness, like any night into the middle of which one woke, seemed everlasting.

At about 1 a.m. a shadowy form stood above me. It was Knollys with a message. A German prisoner had volunteered the information that an enemy counter-attack was to take place at dawn. As there was danger of its developing on our right flank, No. 3 Company had been warned to be ready to support No. 1. With a guide, my platoon sergeant and an orderly, I proceeded to No. 1 to make arrangements with Craigie in case the attack should include his company's front.

Enemy shelling had begun again and through it we passed on our way to No. 1 Company Headquarters. It was something to be on the move, however, with an object in view. It was the road that the enemy was shelling, and down this we had to go or get completely lost in a maze of shell holes. After a certain distance we struck a point from which a white tape led directly to Company Headquarters. This we followed with some difficulty, for it was cut at certain points and stained with mud. After a walk that seemed longer than it actually was we reached Company Headquarters. It was a relief to get under cover and linger there while I listened to instructions from Craigie. Three

Verey lights fired along the ground was to be the signal that support was needed.

I finished my cigarette. I tucked the strap of my " tin " helmet under my chin, and then out again into a dark and dangerous world.

After a few minutes the guide suddenly announced that he had lost the tape. Where were we? We did not know. In vain we stared into the darkness. What could it reveal since the day itself could show nothing. How long had we been on the way? We stood irresolute. The air fanned our cheeks. Skyline and middle distance to left and right, before and behind, flashed and winked to gun and star-shell. We were completely lost. Oh, yes, the stars. Tricky though—this front was pretty ragged. Tentatively we stepped out, very slowly—a super blind man's buff—we walked and walked, every now and then looking down to find no tape. A shadow loomed. What was it? It turned out to be No. 1 Company Headquarters. We had made a complete circle in No Man's Land. How near to the

German lines had we come?

We kept the blessed tape in view the next time, and finally reached the road, which was being thumped as heavily as ever. With great good luck we got safely back to our slit.

Day broke, with no signal from No. 1 Company and no enemy attack.

The morning passed quietly. An enemy aeroplane flying overhead was shelled; our "archies," bursting in the sky with a snuffed sound, looked like jellyfish.

At noon we were heavily shelled for twenty minutes or so with 5.9's, one shell following another at about ten seconds' interval and bursting ten to twenty yards beyond. We crouched in the bottom of the slit waiting for the shell that would land on top of us. A splinter struck softly into the mud next to me and I had missed a "blighty" by an inch.

4

That night I changed places with Knollys and the next night the Battalion was relieved

by the 1st Essex (29th Division). These
reliefs were devilish. The combination of
black night, "uncertain" shelling, guides
missing the way, duckboards along the
routes shelled to bits in places making the
going difficult, and feeling the responsibility
of getting the men out without casualties—
and something of the nightmare it was may be
imagined. Those were days of open war-
fare as regards getting up to and back from
the front line.

Slowly the men were assembled near
Cannes Farm. A "whizz-bang" chipping
its corner covered me with dust and plaster
and my orderly thought I was a casualty.

With our backs to the enemy we moved in
single file down the slippery duckboards.
We reached White Hope Corner, where tea
was served to the men. At Luneville Farm
we entrained, and on the hard wood floor
of my truck I slept the sleep of complete
exhaustion. One hour in twenty-four had
been my average in the line. At 5.40 a.m.
we arrived at Proven. Dazed with insufficient
rest I entered a world of endless slumber

as I crawled into my sleeping bag.

5

Two days later I found myself alone in the mess playing Debussy's " Petite Suite " on the gramophone. In the camp there was the sudden roll of a drum and in the near distance the puff-puff of a train engine. Both failed to interrupt but fitted into the melody itself, which, it amused me to fancy, was my own reaction to the two . . .

The attack on the 20th, regarded as a complete success, had for us a further significance in the rumour that we too would soon be used. Meanwhile we enjoyed the brief security of life behind the line. One day Craigie and I lunched with Orpen at Cassell —a memento of which I still maintain in the impromptu " pen and ink " done on the menu and carefully carried away by me, but which I remember more distinctly for the pretty girl behind the high desk in the restaurant, reported to be engaged to an officer in the Flying Corps. Years afterwards I returned to this primitive hotel to wonder at the charm it had held for me and the positive comfort it had suggested. To wonder, too, what had happened to the girl. But these little excursions, with their tiny tastes of peace, left one disgruntled and unhappy. Unconsciously we reach a level and should stick to it.

Although rumour was confirmed and the Battalion did go over the top, the event coincided with my being sent away on a course in Scouting, Observation and Sniping at Vardencourt, so that I missed the battle.

6

We were billeted in an early eighteenth century château of simple charm, and all enjoyed the course as a respite from war. The days were warm with the scent of cut hay and dry leaves, and after parade we ate apples and dozed against hayricks. At night all the perfume of high noon hung on the air. In the early mornings the dew on the grass shimmered rich as tinsel on a

Christmas tree. Soon it turned cold and rainy, and we, who lived with our cheeks to the weather, felt the change more than most people.

By the middle of October the course was drawing to a close and I got leave to return a day earlier than the others. It was mental luxury to be alone, and travelling independently gave one the illusion that the war was over.

A man in the village with a very second-hand car drove me to Amiens for twenty francs. Passing some German prisoners (there was a camp of them in our vicinity) I pointed them out.

" Ils ne m'intéressent pas ! " he said and so ended all conversation, as we rattled along a road that badly needed repair.

Amiens was depressing. I missed the colour and movement the British and French armies had supplied the year before. Since the German retirement in the spring, Amiens had lain too far behind the lines to remain a place for short leave. I sat in a restaurant near the station, waiting for the time my train was due to leave.

"Amiens is empty," I said to the propriétaire.

At that he became communicative. Last year, he told me, during the Battle of the Somme, thirty Frenchmen had made his café a rendezvous. All had been in the habit of turning up at it while on short leave, and this they had attempted to obtain on Sunday evenings, that they might be sure of finding each other. So it was, with battery or battalion not so very far away, that these officers had come for an hour, a drink and a chat, and then back to their units. But he (the propriétaire) had acted, throughout the long battle of the Somme, as host to a gradually diminishing number. It had been a process of elimination and each Sunday found one or more absent. One of the original thirty gone—killed, wounded or missing. Each week thus had seen one disposed of, while someone who knew would tell the others what had happened to him.

They would talk of him a little, wondering perhaps the while who would be the next

to go, until the following Sunday when
there would be another missing. So it had
gone, until only one was left. One only to
sit in silence or drink his porto with but the
propriétaire to talk to. And then a week
passed, then another, and finally a great
many, without his turning up again. He,
too, had become a casualty, but there remained no one to talk about him and no one
who knew what his end had been.

A real Suicide Club it was, thought I.

Pre-ordained, this compulsory traveller
entered his railway coach. The train slid
smoothly out of Amiens. I was alone in
my carriage and opened the window to
remove the damp smell. Settling myself, I
looked out until the short October day had
drawn to an abrupt close. . . .

7

I rejoined the Battalion, to listen to fragmentary accounts of a battle done in pouring
rain. Four officer casualties—instinctively,
I am ashamed to say, I calculated how that

would place me on the " leave roster." The officer who had taken my place as Intelligence Officer had been shot through the head.

The Battalion lined the road, cheering the Duke of Connaught as he inspected the Division. On the right of the line were the officers, N.C.O.'s and men who had been decorated, mentioned, or recommended in the last " push." As he shook each one by the hand, I wished that I too had a medal.

Paris leave, though expected, came with a relish too great for words. Every minute from the time I left the Battalion was conscious and measured joy. Nor could I have felt fitter, and I entered the train in the evening an anticipatory and privileged being. Sitting up in a day coach all night was no hardship under such conditions. I sat in a corner of the carriage next the window. When we had reached Boulogne three members of a theatrical troupe entered our carriage—two women and a man. One woman was very handsome and I hoped she would sit next to me. She did. During the long night I woke from a fitful doze with an inordinate desire to speak to her. I had not spoken to a woman for months. The green shade had been drawn over the light and we were in semi-darkness. She was sleeping soundly and opened her eyes with a look of wonder. We talked in animated whispers, this strange young woman, whom I never again would see, and I. In the morning, by way of bidding her good-bye, I shook everyone by the hand.

*   *

*

Chapter VII

I

TRAINS ! French trains ! Will they forever remind me of the war ? Every train that I was in those days took me to or from the front. I watched the smoke from the engine drift into separate wisps that looked like shrapnel bursts. Leaning back in my seat, I felt myself being carried along by destiny itself.

The drums reminded me that I was back again, feeling, in the process of a slight readjustment, unreality in the midst of the greatest reality.

While I was away the Battalion had moved by route march from Ypres to the Somme. The day after my rejoining the march continued—a ten mile trek to Houvin-Houvigneul. A halt of two days and then fifteen miles to Bailleulval. The next day nine miles due east to Courcelles le Comte. What was the " big idea " ? We were told.

A surprise attack the following morning on the Cambrai front. If it was not a surprise to the enemy, it certainly was a surprise to us. If a success, we were to be used to exploit the " break through."

We were impressed with fragmentary reports that proclaimed an advance of two and a half miles and the successful use of tanks which had cleared the way for the infantry.

We had plenty of time to think it over.

We were to proceed to Boulencourt by 'buses. From 8 p.m. until 2 a.m. we waited at the embussing point. The sky, which had been cloudy for many a day, cleared for a space and the night was fully decorated with moon and stars.

The 'buses came at last and at 5.30 a.m. we arrived and went into huts. What was going to happen? All day we remained apprehensively at Boulencourt. I was one of so many that a sense of individual danger was lost. Death would be pure accident. No bullet be *intended* for me. One's mind dodged the issue. You did not think of it. *It thought of you.* That was it. It considered

you bodily ; pinning you to earth ; running
you down. For we were certain—I was
certain—to go into battle. What was that
silly line in a story ? It made me think of
a battle as something so romantic as to be
harmless. The man is in love and the girl
has just admitted that she loves him. And
there in the valley below, " The earth opens
and shuts," and so forth. " What's that ? "
cries the girl. " That ! " says the man.
" That's only a battle. You love me ! "
It had so impressed my young imagination
when I read it that I had reacted sentimentally
to the idea of battle ever since.

2

We were in the area of battle. It was here
that British troops had so recently overrun
the impregnable Hindenburg line. The
tracks of the tanks that had flattened some
six aprons of barbed wire could be seen. In
their wake the infantry had followed. All
very neatly done. No artillery preparation.
Few shell holes. Little bloodshed. Many

prisoners. Just a nice clean battle.

We were billeted in a deep dugout. Twenty-four steps. Very safe. In the trench a tank had been stuck, its nose perpendicular in the air—looking a clumsy, helpless thing.

At Flesquières I saw the five tanks, knocked out at point-blank range by a single German gunner major, as they had come over the crest. He was eventually killed, but he had been responsible for holding up the centre of the attack.

The battle had drifted to a finish. The Germans were shelling Anneux. The next day we were to take over the line in front of Anneux and facing Fontaine. Cambrai looked ridiculously within reach. Bourlon Wood, half British and half German, presented an inscrutable appearance. It was too late. We should not be used now. Again I was to miss a battle. On the way back the moon was setting in a sky of violet.

The next day was windy. The clouds had a smudged look as though a dirty finger

had rubbed their edges. Towards evening
the wind died out like the end of a long sigh
and the day was still. Without moon and
stars the night was black and threatened rain.

3

I had met the Battalion with the guides,
but the Commanding Officer was nowhere to
be seen. I found " Billy " though, who was
much excited. He told me what was up, but
I could not take it in. His announcement
affected me physically before I had mentally
grasped it. I felt it like a shock, like a blow,
turning me sick. The Battalion was to
attack the following morning. Once the
words had been formulated and the brain
had recorded and repeated them there
occurred an emotional ebb, leaving the
system drained. Gradually I rallied to the
fact itself, inevitable. All this within the
space of a few seconds. I had morally run
away, fallen, picked myself up, while remaining steadfastly on one spot. But Billy
had disappeared. There was no communi-

cating one's feeling to him. Something of his hysteria permeated, as though he had meant to frighten me. A brave man, he had lost his nerve. And then a strange exultation rose within me. That this could be happening to *me!* In the wake of this emotion I moved in a dream. Something told me it was best to remain in a kind of dream. . . .

The Battalion was in the line. The last Company Commander had reported his relief complete.

The Commanding Officer told me to get some sleep. I looked at him, for it seemed to me I was seeing him for the first time, so kind and quietly human he had become.

It was about four in the morning when the Commanding Officer himself woke me. The candles, stuck in bottles on the table, burned as straight as on any altar. Each step up the twenty-two of the dugout was a conscious movement. Now we were at the entrance. The night was still, breathless. It had been raining. The air on our faces left a moisture. The ground was soggy and the going difficult. The mud stuck to our boots until we were walking on huge pads.

We came upon No. 1 Company—mutes and shadows and something more than men.

The Commanding Officer went down a dugout to have a last word with " Mary " Bowes-Lyon while I remained and joked with the two subalterns. How is it one can jest at such a time? It's a question of tuning up. Laughter is the loophole through which joy enters the soul.

We were slipping along again. An interminable walk to go a few yards. But we had missed No. 2 Company and were out in No Man's Land heading for the enemy.

We made for the road which divided the Battalion. By the time we had reached Nos. 3 and 4 Companies they were forming up. Sinister shadows filling the gloom, as silent as the night itself, only the immense discipline of the Brigade of Guards kept one from remembering they were men cold and wet and dulled with fear.

Jack Hughes was calm and cool, and Carrington interested and conscientious.

Young Hanham, aged nineteen, was lost, but we found him on our way to No. 2 Company near the wreck of a British plane.

On recrossing the road we found " Nibs " Beaumont-Nesbitt, elated but not excited, full of a fine exultation that inspired everyone. I will never forget him.

Dawn was showing " dirty white " when we got back to Battalion Headquarters.

At 6.20 our barrage came down and while I thought of the Battalion as a unit, five hundred men had begun their perilous progress towards the enemy trenches.

4

I stood with my observers on high ground near the entrance to the dugout. I was thrilled. The sound of battle was in the air—a light cannonade on both sides and a great rattle of machine-gun fire coming from the German lines. A shell bursting near us came, so to speak, to punctuate the excitement I felt. I was safe. One of too many for mishap to single out.

But our eyes could not pierce the mist that hung over the battlefield. For purpose of observation our position was useless. Soon I received orders to proceed to the foot of the village and, obtaining touch with the Companies, to relay messages back to Battalion Headquarters. I started out with six observers, cutting across the field behind Nos. 1 and 2 Companies. We passed Sergeant Rhodes, V.C., D.C.M., mortally wounded, being carried back on a stretcher. A fine big man, but lying deep in the stretcher and covered with a blanket, he seemed immeasurably to have shrunk. Only his head, immense and white, like an indomitable will appeared to keep life in him. But soon he would be a corpse, all his great strength and courage were ebbing fast.

I questioned him, but although conscious, he could say little. Poor man, I was thinking, poor man ! It had only been a few months ago that he had captured an enemy pill-box single-handed. Among his prisoners had been an artillery forward observing officer.

The full orchestra of battle was on. The
air seemed alive with invisible wires being
twanged, while the earth was thumped and
beaten.

The bullets zipped, whizzed, whistled,
spun, sung, and sighed according to their
proximity and their point of flight. They
constituted in reality the spray off the wave
of lead being poured into Nos. 1 and 2
Companies, although I scarcely realised this
at the time.

We had reached the foot of the village
without a casualty. I was standing on
ground newly won. To my left and right
stretched deserted enemy entrenchments.
Near me lay two wounded Grenadiers. One
was in a ditch full of water. They were remarkably quiet. I felt I should get them back
somehow, but there were no stretcher
bearers about.

Out of the house next to which I was standing appeared three Germans. They were
holding up their hands. One had his foot in a
bandage and was being helped along by the
others. They looked frightened and miserable

While they are chattering in German, a wounded Grenadier turned up, quite off his head.

"That's all right, sir," he addressed me. "I'll kill them."

"I wouldn't do that," I remonstrated.

"Oh, that's quite all right. You just leave them to me." He threatened them with his rifle. The wounded German started to whimper and shuffled off.

The Grenadier followed, herding his little party together. He used his rifle like a shepherd's staff. Could he have been a shepherd in civilian life ? They disappeared in the direction of an out-house. Whatever happened to them ? They were not heading strictly for the British lines.

Another small party of prisoners appeared with a wounded Grenadier as escort. He was dazed and shaking with fright.

"Take a door off this house and have these prisoners carry back this wounded man." But he did not understand.

The prisoners stood nervously about wishing to be gone. I showed them what I

wanted done and they complied with alacrity.
Soon they were off, carrying the wounded
Grenadier. It must have been a heavy load.
I could not help fearing they would drop him
half way in their eagerness to get out of
danger. But if they had any thought of
doing so it was intercepted by a German
shell which burst in their midst after they
had gone two hundred yards.

More prisoners turning up, removed
another door from a house, on which they
placed the man lying in the ditch of water.

Suddenly a large group of Germans
approached. Their leader was a big man
and the rest followed with a martial tread
that contrasted oddly with their upraised
hands and white handkerchiefs, energetically
waved by some. One or two dodged into
houses, but the rest marched on until they
had reached us. The big man addressed me
and I felt like a traffic policeman as I pointed
to the British lines and watched them hurry
off.

Messages arrived from Nos. 3 and 4 Companies. They had captured their objectives,

they were held up by heavy German machine-gun fire, they had suffered considerably and were in need of reinforcements. No word from either Nos. 1 or 2 Companies —a bad sign.

The Commanding Officer turned up. I saluted as though on parade.

He looked anxious.

" We must go up and see what is happening."

Together we proceeded up the main street of Fontaine-Notre-Dame, down which machine-gun bullets were pouring with the volume of water from a fire-hose. We hugged the houses to minimize the danger of being hit.

We reached the cross-roads and I marvelled that a man could get so far and remain alive. We were in the van of the battle. It seemed a miracle had happened to me.

Knollys greeted us. His Company Commander had been wounded. He was holding his position with about forty men and one machine-gun. It was almost all that was left of the Battalion. Nos. 1 and 2 Com-

panies had disappeared into the blue. They
had been, as a matter of fact, wiped out. All
officers (including both Company Com-
manders killed) both Sergeant-Majors, and
all Sergeants casualties, and two-thirds of
the men. Knollys was not certain but he
thought No. 4 Company was somewhere up
on the left.

On the extreme left of Knollys' position
the road turned sharp to the right. Up this
I was sent to reconnoitre, and never had a
road seemed more empty, nor I more solitary.

I found Carrington with about thirty men,
all that was left of No. 4 Company. He
looked exhausted. He was standing beside
a German field gun. We should have put it
out of commission.

Our consultation was interrupted by the
appearance of a tank. It stopped, and out of
it an officer descended.

" Do you want me any more ? "

" No." I felt as though I were dismissing
a taxi.

He climbed back into the tank and
down the street it waddled away.

We occupied a difficult position. The road to our rear joined with the left flank of No. 3 Company. We stood at the junction of the two other roads, one of which led to the station and the other in the direction of Bourlon Wood. The 1st Coldstream were somewhere on our left. A wide gap divided us, a gap impossible to bridge.

Suddenly to our right we saw the enemy attacking down the main road that led to the centre of No. 3 Company's position. We were well placed to enfilade, which we did with a will. We watched the Germans being beaten back, holding up their arms before their faces as though warding off blows from sticks and stones.

With that attack driven back we thought of No. 3 Company as secure. The men were posted to overlook the roads. We had no thought of our rear. I sent a runner with a message giving our position.

5

I had whisky in my water bottle and some

milk chocolate in my pockets. Some twenty yards below the junction of roads was a house. On the side facing No. 3 Company's position ran a wall enclosing a small yard. Carrington and I entered the house. A house recently evacuated; chairs and table and everything just as they had been left. We ate some chocolate and took a pull at my water bottle. We said little— one or two irrelevant remarks. Our situation was awkward, to say the least. Sixty men with both flanks in the air cannot hold a village against a strong and inevitable counter-attack.

I caught sight of my face in a mirror. It was pink and normal. I had not taken in the seriousness of our position. I was still in a kind of a dream. A mental smoke-screen obscured my vision.

Even the sergeant's astonishing announcement reached me dimly, "Germans are coming up be'ind!"

By no selective reasoning did I find myself, with revolver drawn, behind the wall, while the others stood in the entrance of the yard.

And to be suddenly shooting at grey uniformed Germans was accompanied by no thrill. How big they were! Was it because he was aiming straight at my head that this German appeared so big? The motion of his rifle coming up to his shoulder increased his stature. My revolver lost power to hurt, for after I had fired the Germans remained in the same position. And yet they were so near it would have seemed impossible to have missed them. (A week before I had hit an envelope at twenty paces.) It did not seem as though I was missing but rather as though my bullets, turning into pellets, were bounding harmlessly off. Nor did the German's rifle seem to function. There was no smoke, no flash, and I heard no bullet whistle uncomfortably close to my head. The whole thing took on the unreality of a " movie " until one of the Germans dropped. It seemed the signal for which his fellows had been waiting, for with one accord they spun round and ran away. I have never seen people run so fast. I can see again that man as he turned the corner, the

play of his big grey legs from hip to knee.
He is gone.

I gazed at Carrington and he at me. It
was from our rear that we had been attacked.
Where is No. 3 Company?

It was the sergeant who showed presence
of mind.

"We must follow."

Someone shouted. "Collect the rest of
the men."

We broke into a run; following in the
wake of the Germans. We passed the
wounded German. He had raised himself
on his elbow and, stretching out a hand, said
something. A plea for mercy, for help?
The bullet had hit the bone below the eye,
leaving a bloody gash.

We reached the bend in the road. This
had been the left of No. 3 Company's
position. Only a dead Grenadier remained.
Did we expect to meet the enemy as we
stopped stock-still at the corner? I expected
nothing. I had ceased to think. It was as
though our legs had outstripped thought.
Time itself had stopped. The surprise

attack, the brief duel, the pursuit, following
in swift succession seemed all to belong to
the same moment. Only now was time
passing. An eternity, while one stood
irresolute, wondering what to do.

"We must cut in be'ind these 'ouses,
otherwise we're lost." It was the sergeant
again who spoke.

It was true enough. We could soon
expect an attack in force, and from several
directions. The rest of the Company had
joined us. Some thirty Britishers in the
village of Fontaine.

The apparently deserted houses seemed
haunted. The windows took on the semblance of glassy eyes. Soon we should be
the victims of a dangerous game of hide and
seek. How many of the enemy were near at
hand, lurking around corners, organizing an
attack? What resistance could we make?
Already the reconnoitring party we had met
must have reported our presence. Soon the
enemy would be upon us in force. These
fears, not voiced, scarcely apprehended,
raced like shadows across the mind. The

men were on the move, quietly and in good order. Once through the first house, I waited to see the last man over the wall into the next garden, terrified now that my back was turned to the enemy: a slow-motion picture could not have expressed my own sensation of movement as we climbed from one garden to another.

6

We were clear of the village. We stood opposite No. 3 and 4 Companies' old positions. A hostile barrage was coming down with some power, but we passed through it with a feeling of comparative safety, now that we were quit of the village itself.

We found the remnant of No. 3 Company reinforced by a company of the 4th Grenadiers. "Cocky" Hoare of the 4th Battalion was much excited. I was surprised at his agitation. He was anticipating a big counter-attack on our very heels. I stayed with him until it occurred to me the Commanding

137

Officer would like to know what had happened to No. 4 Company.

Experience, at first stimulating, ends by draining the system. Through the high storm of enemy shelling I passed, with any capacity for registering further emotion at last microscopically diminished. I felt no fear because I could feel nothing more.

Slithering down the steep and muddy flight of stairs into the dim interior of Battalion Headquarters' dugout was a purely mechanical performance, and its shadowy occupants unreal. Its gloom and earthen smell reminded my subconscious self of former rest and security, which acted soporifically upon me and, at the end of my narrative, I fell forward on to the table into a sleep more profound and dreamless than any I had ever known.

I woke into a strange world. The events of the preceding hours rushed kaleidoscopically upon me, leaving me to fit myself, like a piece in a picture puzzle, into my immediate surroundings.

The Battalion was soon to move. Billy

was sitting with his head in his hands saying, " Oh, my head ! Oh, my head ! "

In the midst of the most acute anxiety, disappointment and distress, the Commanding Officer had patience to repeat for the *n*th time, " Poor Billy ! "

The Adjutant and the Padre returned from a final futile hunt for the bodies of " Nibs " and " Mary." " Missing, believed killed " they will remain until the end of time, with the rest of a generation missing.

A miserable and stricken little family, the survivors of the 3rd Battalion left the " line."

7

The next day—at a time when I was well able to appreciate it—my leave to England came through.

I made a wide circle to avoid a particular point being shelled ; fearful, now that I was temporarily a detached human, of being hit.

From the transport lines I walked until I had reached a point in the road where vehicular traffic began.

Soon the headlights of a car, turning a slight corner, threw stark trees into spectral relief. It was a sign for which I was waiting and I placed myself tentatively in its path.

It came to a halt.

" May I have a lift ? "

" Arras suit you ? "

I jumped in. The car, picking up, jolted slowly along a bad road made worse by darkness.

I looked back, always eager for impressions at heightened moments. The sky-line flashed and turned black, like a wink. I turned and sat staring ahead into the night feeling

" . . . content beyond content
That hath not any room for betterment."

At Arras the man in the front seat next to the driver got out. I discovered to my slight dismay that he was a Major-General.

He very genially invited me to dine with the 9th Divisional Headquarters.

My old Division ! I thought of this rather odd coincidence as I sat with the

junior officers, and then I thought of
Kimberly. Two and a half years before,
when I had dined with the officers of his
battalion, he had intrigued me—as people
will who reflect oneself. I had sat next to
him on that particular occasion and either
because he had had a drink or two or because
he found me responsive, he had told me how
he hated the war. It bored and sickened and
frightened him. From every angle it re-
volted him. Before the war he had been the
Paris correspondent of a newspaper. He
loved Paris as English and Americans love it,
for its cafés, its " atmosphere," the sense of
delightful detachment it alone can give. His
sensitive face, dark with soldiering, took on
a lively look as he allowed himself to con-
template a return to his former existence.
But soon again his eyes flashed metallic
behind his glasses. My gaze wandered from
him to the adjutant and I considered how
different two men could be as I observed
" Blank," tall, athletic and handsome and
every inch a soldier.

Two and a half years had elapsed and the

bloody battle of Loos and the bloodier
battles of the Somme and 3rd Ypres had
been fought !

It was purely perfunctorily that I asked the
man next to me :

" Did you by chance ever run across a man
named Kimberly in your regiment ? "

" Kimberly ? " And I looked up, for his
voice gave the name sudden distinction.
" Yes.   Fine officer.   Still with his battalion.
Got the M.C. the other day."   (I will finish
this story now.)

A year later, July 1918, we were relieved
in the line by the Argyll and Sutherland Highlanders, and again I asked after Kimberly.

" Oh ! " said the officer taking over from
us, " Kimberly ? "   (He too gave the name
distinction—a vocal decoration, as it were.)
" He's still with the battalion.   Refused all
sorts of cushy jobs.   Has a D.S.O. and
M.C.   Wonderful soldier ! "

It was, therefore, with real eagerness that I
asked about Kimberly a year after the war,
when I met Ian Hay at luncheon.   His

eyes took on a far-away look. The distance their light travelled seemed to date the occurrence itself.

"He was killed. Just at the end. Wonderful soldier."

8

The spray from two destroyers escorting us across the Channel, broke white and as high as explosives at the front, and I reflected on this expensive protection given lives as cheap as ours.

*   *

*

Chapter VIII

I

THE weather was freezing. Only on retiring (because of a hot water bottle) were
my feet warm. From early morning until
late at night they were two blocks of ice.
The thickest Jaeger socks were so much
tissue paper against such cold, and in the
officers' mess a single stove gave out as much
warmth as a candle. Even dancing, which
we occasionally did to keep warm, did no
good. The chill of winter was insistent and
the tile floor of a French kitchen had the cold
surface of a layer of ice.

All day it snowed. The moon came out to
shine on trees covered with crystal to blend,
it would seem, with the snow.

The following day our resourceful and
indefatigable Commanding Officer organised
a snowball fight with the Irish Guards. But
he was right ; keep the men occupied and
you kept them from going stale.

I developed a cold. It grew into a cough. The cough got worse. I ought to have " gone sick." I saw the Medical Officer (American attached) every day; why didn't he order me to go sick? If I had I should have recovered and would soon be returned back on duty; but if not I should become really ill and that would mean hospital and then, if I was lucky, England. Did I really want to get out of it all or was it because of the cold that my morale was low? Two days in bed and I would have been rid of this cough, but that always looked as though one were trying to avoid parade. This, it seemed, was a vicious circle.

Carrington returned from leave. He had a D.S.O. for Fontaine. A sergeant in his company got hold of an extra ration or two of rum the morning of the attack. He went wild. He stripped himself naked to the waist and led attacks into several houses, killing a number of the enemy single-handed. He got a D.C.M.

While I was on leave the big German counter-attack at Cambrai took place. The

Guards Division, then in rest or reserve, was
called on to fill a big gap left by the precipit-
ate retirement of another division. It saved
the day. " Crawley " de Crespigny (so
gossip had it) mounted his charger and rode
up under fire to reconnoitre the ground for
his brigade. Paton won the first officer
Victoria Cross of the war for the Grenadiers.
Exposing himself recklessly in full view of
the enemy and under a murderous machine-
gun fire he ran from trench to trench to
encourage odd groups of men to hold on to
their positions. For a time he bore a
charmed life—long enough, it seems, to have
accomplished his purpose—and then he fell
mortally wounded.

The weather remained icy and my cough
got worse. I should be really ill. Did I
derive comfort from the fact ? I would like
to say I did not. No one seemed to bother,
however. The daughter of the old girl in
whose house I was billeted brought me
something warm to drink when she heard me
coughing in the night.

Christmas night. Champagne was drunk

by the Battalion Headquarters mess. We became flushed and merry—purely artificially so—all very jolly.

" Hell ! I *must* be ill."

The first day of the new year came pale as death. The trees looked very black against the snow. The ruts in the roads were frozen hard. In the process of shaving, one's fingers became so cold that one had to dip them in the hot water to be able to go on. We bought a tree from a farmer to use as kindling wood. The men tore off every loose plank in their huts for the same purpose. Very much against regulations, but who could have stopped them ?

At night I discussed books with " the daughter of the house."   She had never been further afield than St. Pol (a town a few miles away), but she was very well informed.

" How is it that you know so much ? "

" Je voyage dans mes livrcs."

A paroxysm of coughing on my part.

" Vous savez, mon pauvre garçon, vous êtes vraiment malade."

" I quite agree."   (England !)

147

In January the Battalion moved up to trenches in front of Arras.

I was left behind until the new unit had taken over the billets and found them " all correct."

It was dark when I left for Arras. Nothing moved on the road. I had to walk—five or six or seven miles? A frequent look over my shoulder as I stumbled on revealed nothing. I moved on automatically, breathing hard and painfully. I would scarcely know when I had reached Arras. There wouldn't be many lights. Interminable! How could anything take so long. What? Was I asleep? Where am I? Oh, yes, Arras. I must get to Arras. God, but I feel groggy.

Outlying houses, like stragglers, appeared in the gloom, and then I was in Arras itself, walking the streets of a town empty of life but for a private soldier or two. It stood only partially destroyed, but the Hôtel de Ville with its fine Gothic façade and the cathedral were among the ruins. I don't know why I thought of this as I sought

Battalion Headquarters. The word periwinkle also suddenly occurred without my
associating the name with its meaning.
" Periwinkle ! " I said out loud. " Periwinkle ! " I announced as I entered the
officers' mess.

" Periwinkle ? " questioned Alec Agar-
Robartes.

" Well, possibly not," I replied. . . .

The next morning the Battalion went into
the line ; fine, deep, well-made trenches.

On our left the Germans were shelling a
large pond frozen over. The crash of the
shell was followed by an immense splitting
of the ice. Quite a magnificent sound.

That night on lying down in the dugout
I started to take off a boot.

" You can't take your boots off."

It was the Commanding Officer who had
spoken.

I looked up. " Why, of course not."

He observed me closely. " You had
better go sick to-morrow morning."

All night in the dugout I tossed and
coughed. I had a high fever, I knew that,

and the pain in my side had increased. Pleurisy no doubt.

I tried to appear sorry to be leaving when I said good-bye to " Bulgy " in the morning, but each step on the duckboards of the long communication trench was sheer joy in spite of the pain in my side. . . .

But I am ill all right. A temperature of 104—not so bad. I am pleased my going sick has been justified. How cool these sheets and how warm these blankets.

And my service jacket on the chair over there. I must get a ribbon sewn on it as soon as possible. A Military Cross won at Cambrai. What for ? I don't know, but I'm glad to have got it. It's such a pretty ribbon. If only I were on the staff I could get a lot of medals ! And no risk involved !

I am lucky. They have pinned a blue paper to the blanket on my bed. This means England. . . .

2

London was like a medieval town those

days, so dimly lighted was it, except of
course for the searchlights. In the old days
(*i.e.*, just before the war) the city had been
light and the sky dark. Now it was the
reverse.

I went to Lady Ridley's, a big house in
Carlton House Terrace turned into a hospital
for officers. (The German Embassy had been
in Carlton House Terrace.) The large rooms
and halls were wards containing rows of
occupied cots. Some of the wounded dated
from Cambrai. Horton of the " Kiddies,"
his arm in a sling, paid me a visit. He had
been hit Fontaine-Notre-Dame day. The
Scots Guards had attempted to link up with
our right flank, but had come under the same
murderous machine-gun fire from La Folie
Wood which had destroyed Nos. 1 and 2
Companies.

It was good to see Father and talk to
him as he sat by my bed while I convalesced.
He was unusually cheerful. His colourful
face beamed down upon me. He expected
great things from America.

" I don't like to think of your going

out again," he said.

" I don't want to go out again."

" But you must do your duty."

" There is talk of their sending twelve officers from the Brigade for propaganda work in the States. It seems to me I am a logical person to go. Anyway, I have applied."

" I hope you are chosen."

" I hope so."

" You will be doing your duty."

" I may be doing more good than getting shot at. I like to think so."

" I am sure of it. I am quite certain of it."

" But when are *you* sailing, Father ? "

" Soon. I shall be there to welcome you —unless by some great chance we go together."

" We'll have some fun on the other side. It's four years since I was in America. I remember telling people when I sailed I would be back in six months."

" You left in April, 1914 ? "

" Yes."

" That's almost exactly four years ago."

"I wonder if I shall remember anything else as easily and pleasantly as that voyage—and for so little reason. Nothing happened. But I was on my own and each day was exactly like the one before—blue and sunny. As we approached Madeira the nights were velvety blue. They were jewelled and precious nights—a still and phosphorous sea and every star out. The stars increase as you go south. The bigger constellations cast reflections thin as gold thread. There was an attractive girl on board with a sense of humour by day and none, thank heaven, by night. The evenings came on us with real enchantment, and looking over the steamer rail, we discussed Life with a capital L. I planned big things. I told her I wanted to *be* somebody, but I was vague about how I was going to accomplish it. She was impressed until I got very tight in Madeira. The inhabitants drink Madeira out of tumblers, and I thought I could do the same. And then I landed at Gibraltar and the girl went on to Italy. I spent a night in Algeciras where there are lovely flowers and a good

hotel and a silly little casino, and from where
you can see the rock of Gibraltar like a
mighty army boot across the bay. In
Seville I saw my first bull-fight and had to
leave because it made me sick, and yet I have
managed a war up to date. How do you
explain that, Father? It's all so long ago
now—that trip, those sunny blue days, and I
a detached and independent human being. I
wonder if I was as happy as I remember to
have been? And will I ever be quite as
happy again? Something tells me I shall
never know such simple and motiveless joy.
The war like a dead weight will hang on long
after it is over. . . . Goodness, how did I
get going like this?" Father was gazing at
me in perplexity and concern.

Then the big German offensive and the
"back to the wall" message from Haig. My
plan to go to the States for propaganda
purposes was rudely interrupted. Every
officer was needed.

I was called to the Orderly Room and
questioned by the Adjutant.

"Have you been passed fit?"

" No sir.   But I feel fit."

Shortly after I was sent out with a draft of officers.

Not before seeing Dorothy once more.

Good old Dorothy ! (What an extraordinary attitude of mind to have toward a young and lovely girl.)

But what was the use of a young and lovely girl ?

She bent over her needlework. And there was her piano, and I suppose if I had looked on the music rack I might have seen

"They are not long, the weeping and the laughter."

Well, they are long enough !

I was certainly not going to ask her to sing it, anyway.

" The days of wine and roses."   Hell ! The song had no reality, and yet it had seemed once to carry a message.   How I had changed.

That booming on one's heart and head, that hammering out of one's sensibilities ! I had become flat and characterless as a silhouette.

" You are very silent." One had to be unusually silent for Dorothy's detached person to take offence. . . .

And Susan !

" Let me know when you get leave."

Leave ! It was so remote, and yet from the moment one had arrived in France it remained uppermost in one's thoughts.

How simply and how effectively Susan struck the right note.

" We shall be at Coombe this Saturday to Monday. I wish you were going to be with us."

" I will think of you so intensely that you *may* feel me near you."

" I shall be glad to leave this mouldy old house."

" I wish I could stop in this mouldy old house."

" With me or without me ? "

" With you and Eddie and the children and anybody else you want."

" You hate going out again ? "

" The idea is repulsive to me. Don't let's think about it—don't let's think at all.

Let's feel. I love you."

" I love my husband."

" I like him too. But he's unworthy of you, and so am I. That starts us equal in your eyes. Choose! But you have, and once a woman makes her choice she stands committed."

" You know women ? "

" Well, I know you, and I should say you're very much a woman."

She held her nose in the air, but she held it prettily.

" When I look into your eyes I want to weep, when I look at your nose I want to laugh, and—when I look at your mouth I want to kiss you."

" What are you looking at now ? "

" Your mouth."

" Here is something for you." She produced a tiny silk American flag. I put it away in the upper left hand pocket of my service jacket.

" And *you* don't think so very much of American men."

" I know one who invited me to his flat

at five in the morning!" she mocked.

"It's not true. But I wish I had made you come. Oh, God! I've got to go. The train leaves in half an hour, and I have to pick up a haversack and so forth. No, don't come with me. I like to think of you last in your own house—mouldy though it may be."

I looked into her eyes—those starry eyes whose gaze travelled far—or seemed to, yet took me with it to its furthest point—or seemed to. Because of the moment's intense reality there was created for me a sense of continuity. I left her house turning over ridiculous plans that belonged to a vague and impossible future but which left me buoyed until some time after the train had slipped quickly out of Waterloo Station.

3

Ah, ha! Jolly old Havre. Sweet spot. You gloomy old s—t house! "I'm tired of carrying this bloody bird!"

There they are again. There they are,

like a couple of automatons. The Commanding Officer and Adjutant. At least they might have been changed, so that one might be sent to the front by a new face. Oh well, what does it matter ?

Guy Westmacott and I walked along the waterfront. Severely wounded once, he was now finally patched up and was out again. Had refused a staff job.

" I think I shall be killed this time," he speculated.

" I knew a man in the ' Gunners '— Barton. He was certain that he was *not* going to be killed, and he was."

" And then there is Pryce ! I bet *he* never thought about death at all."

In the battle of Armentières, when the Portuguese broke and ran (it is said they killed motor-cyclists to get away the quicker) and thereby left a big gap, the Regiment had got its second officer V.C. But what a V.C. ! It would take all the blood-red ribbon in England turned into tape to properly measure such courage. The 4th Guards Brigade had been put in to fill the gap. It was brigaded with the thirty-first Division, commonly known as the " thirty-worst," so it had to do most of the work. It was ordered to hold out until the Australians had established a new line to its rear. It did. Dwindling away in the process to companies of twenty to thirty strong. The 4th Grenadier Guards lost every officer except its Commanding Officer and Adjutant. This was First Ypres all over again.

Captain Pryce, M.C., commanded a company in this battalion. He held out against overwhelming odds for two days and two nights. By noon the second day he had run out of ammunition and his company numbered eighteen instead of one hundred and fifty. He was entirely surrounded. He had been enfiladed all day by machine-guns. The Germans in front could no longer fire without the risk of shooting Germans behind Pryce's position. They thought they were being held up by at least a battalion. It was now a question of minutes. Pryce did not surrender. He did not even wait to be massacred. He stepped out of his trench and led a bayonet charge against the enemy. He was last seen being clubbed to death by Germans. A wounded corporal lay in a shell hole and crawled back during the night, the sole survivor. He told the story about Captain Pryce.

I felt quite a " vieux client de la maison " as we sat down in Tortoni for dinner and a bottle of vintage wine. . . .

On our way up the line we passed a night in Rouen. We arrived in the early morning. Walking around its streets I saw a very pretty girl near the cathedral. One did not expect to " pick up " someone early in the morning—that kind was not about. She was so respectable looking that I was slightly surprised to see her smile. We spoke and I found her so attractive that I asked if we could meet that evening. I felt rather flattered when she said " Yes."

" A quelle heure ? "

" Vers six heures ? "

" Et l'adresse, Mademoiselle ? "

I thought about her all day. On the way up the line one thought exclusively of women. It was pleasant to have a particular one to concentrate upon.

At six I turned up at our rendezvous. The bell was answered at once. I was in a house of ill-repute. Impossible! There must be some mistake. But no.

"Entrez, Monsieur!"

"Mademoiselle Hélène?"

"Mais oui, Monsieur, mademoiselle est là."

I saw her. I remonstrated with her. She was a different class.

"Voyons, Monsieur, il faut gagner de l'argent lors qu'on peut."

4

The Battalion was bivouacked in a wood. A very leafy and pleasant wood, for the Battalion was in rest.

Bulgy was out-Bulgying himself, and training continued so strenuous that everyone longed to get up into the trenches. Perhaps that is what he wanted. Perhaps that is how morale is achieved. I know he thought me very idle, but I was sick to death of parades. To watch the men do physical exercises gave me positive nausea.

Into the line we finally went and there followed what was known as a tour of the trenches. Four days in the front line, four days in support, and four days in reserve *ad infinitum*.

There were diversions. I met an intelligent and pleasant officer in the Irish Guards, whom we were relieving, who introduced me to Housman's " Epitaph on an Army of Mercenaries." It might have been written for the Old Contemptibles.

" These . . .
　Followed their mercenary calling
　And took their wages and are dead."
　．　．　．　．　．　．　．　．　．　．
" What God abandoned, these defended
　And saved the sum of things for pay."

They are all gone. Yet does the Battalion persist a unit, a power, a continued and continuing reality. Its composition changes, men fall by the way, and they are replaced and it remains. One thinks of it as the same. The 3rd Battalion at Loos, on the Somme, at Ypres, at Cambrai, at Arras—and Waterloo, too, for that matter.

We had a short discussion, this Irish Guardsman and I. (I wish I could remember his name, for he helped me.) He echoed my subconscious. He put into words what I had felt and was groping for.

" In the beginning war is adventure. Then comes war-weariness, a period of adjustment. You stick it or give up. The third phase is an acceptance, a resignation, and a surrender to faith. The brave man is the man who gets through to the third phase."

" ' The brave man is not he who feels no fear, but he whose noble soul its fear subdues,' " I quoted. . . .

There were other episodes. A shell splinter smashing my field glasses and another in my box respirator suffice so far as " narrow escapes " are concerned.

There was the slight incident of the

young American officer attached to us. His delighted incredulity at the quiet of the trenches. He had expected an almost ceaseless rain of bursting shells. He became quite sprightly about it. War was child's play, he intimated. I watched his change of expression when they carried down the dead body of the American M.O. (the back of his head blown off by the only shell that day).

After that we had a battalion attached to us and one night when I was out in No Man's Land doing a patrol we were shot at, not by the Germans, but the Americans. After all, it was our fault for keeping too close to our own wire and I don't blame them for mistaking our shadowy figures for the enemy. I should certainly have felt the same my first time in the line. . . .

Once, at "details," Sargent, who was painting in that part of the front, dined with us. He had just come back from the States where he had painted Wilson. He told us that after painting the portrait of the President his friends said, "But we don't know him now any better than we did

before." " Neither do I ! " replied Sargent.
He said he wanted to paint a picture of
American troops relieving British in the
line.

5

In the original " line up " I was left out.
We were over-officered and so, for the
scheduled attack, young officers were chosen
among those who had not been " blooded " ;
I was to remain with details. Later, the
Commanding Officer decided to have a
reserve officer with Brigade Headquarters
and so I got as far as our jumping-off
positions, and was able to see my company
" off."

It was about one in the morning when
we reached the line. It had been a lovely
moonlight night, then it had showered,
and in the very early morning, a thick fog
wrapped the earth as in cotton wool.

The men, who had had what little sleep
they could, took their ration of rum, and
breakfast, consisting of tea and bacon, at
3 a.m., and finally at 4.30 fixed bayonets

and stood to arms. The attack was set for 4.55 a.m., that being about the time day peeped on the morning of August 21st, 1918.

There was no artillery preparation as a prelude to this battle—only a curtain of fire due to come down and precede our advancing waves at zero hour—so that there was a very real lull before the storm.

The night had been exceptionally quiet. With battle at hand it assumed as usual an ominous silence. And quite right too—the day had something to reveal. Only an occasional shell came to disturb the almost perfect calm that reigned, and served but to intensify the stillness. Even the men spoke little, and then in whispers, like people in church, with death at the altar.

From 4.30 onwards the time went leaden-footed. Glancing at my watch became a continuous and methodical performance. From eight minutes to five on it remained before me. At seven minutes to five only the distant pup-pup-pup of a machine-gun could be heard. Then silence absolute, a breathless hush. You could have heard a tear splash. Six minutes to five and one felt the proximity of the hour like a near presence. Suddenly a gun, like the mighty slamming of a door in a sleeping house, broke the stillness. The hour arranged by fiend and man had come and hell stepped up on to the earth. Every one of the myriad guns crowding the area behind took up the signal and belched forth fire and noise. The battle had begun. Our objective lay south. The Battalion fell in and marched down a road parallel to the enemy lines until they had reached a certain point, where they left-faced. I went a short distance with the company and saying good-bye, stood and watched the men as they were quickly mixed with mist.

I returned to Brigade Headquarters, which was receiving its ration of shells.

Later in the morning I stood in the sunken road listening to fragmentary accounts of the attack from stretcher bearers and walking wounded. Duff Cooper had distinguished himself by taking his company objective with a platoon, and had followed this up by capturing a machine-gun and twenty Germans single-handed, through the simple method of addressing them in their own language. "Kommen Sie heraus—keine waffen." Out they had come and very much astonished to see a single Englishman brandishing a revolver. "If only they had known that I could not have hit one of them!" observed Duff afterwards. But he got a D.S.O. and deserved a V.C.

One day previous to this he had been discovered under very heavy shell fire reading "The Decline and Fall of the Roman Empire." Of quiet and scholarly stuff are soldiers made. "Soldiers are dreamers."

6

Attack and counter-attack, and the third day the offensive continued. The Intelligence Officer had been detailed to guide tanks, and as that was to keep him occupied all night, I was sent for to take his place. I went down the road over which the

Battalion had marched two days before and reached Battalion Headquarters at about 2.30 a.m. I found all the Company officers with the Commanding Officer poring over a map.

At 4.0 a.m. we "went over." Our jumping-off position was this side of a single-track railway which the Boches were shelling intermittently. Four o'clock was before dawn so the battle began by moonlight. . . .

"The new moon glinting hard on eyes
    Wide with insanities."

(Only this time it was the old moon !)

At 4 a.m. our barrage came down and on the other side of the railway Hunland flashed and blazed (like a storm on a stage splendidly exaggerated) as shell after shell screeched closely overhead and pitched and burst on the ground beyond. The next minute we were engulfed in the German counter-barrage. Thunder and lightning concentrating on one spot ! I was showered with dirt, which hit me like spray from a wave breaking against the side of a ship. I slipped into a slit and found myself jammed against two private soldiers. It was very shallow and from the waist up we stood exposed. It seemed impossible to remain unhit as we waited.

We constituted the second wave of the attack and were not due to go over until zero plus twenty minutes.

Suddenly there came a shock, like a mighty blow on the head, and everything turned black. I came to, with my head spinning and my ears buzzing as though they held two huge and angry bees. I wasn't hit, a lucky escape, but when I looked at my watch and said " It's time to go over," the next man to me replied, " I've lost the use of my arm." I must have been dazed for I couldn't understand what he meant. How can one lose the use of one's arm? Slowly I realised he had been hit. I noticed then that the man next to him was also wounded.

Hoisting myself out I went along to get

the other men up and over, but the first
group ten yards further on paid no attention
to my command. All were casualties. An
officer wounded in the back, and five men
killed and wounded.

The officer was rather dramatic, a thing
unusual at the front, where people die quite
simply.

" I'm dying," he said. " I have a letter
here from my mother I haven't had a
chance to read."

I couldn't think what to say, so just said
" Really ! ", a most inadequate remark. I
got him up and we carried him to a dugout.
I felt relieved to get into it. But only a
minute and then I went out and over.

I felt the deepest relief at being on the
other side of the railway and actually in
motion.

The front companies had cleared the way.
There was no opposition for us. No enemy
except groups of prisoners—an officer.
One poor devil kept making a jerking
movement upwards with his hands to attract
my attention, repeating, " Me Saxe, me Saxe,

me no Prusse, me Saxe ! " He had evidently heard that the only people we really had it in for were the Prussians. I tried to reassure him but he only went monotonously on.

We reached the Company objective. Our left flank was in the air, and we were enfiladed.

I started back to Battalion Headquarters to report, and almost ran into a wounded German crawling out of a shell hole. He was stark naked. He had a deep scalp wound from which blood had flowed and congealed, covering his face like a red mask. He could not see and had lost his sense of balance. There were no clothes near him. He had not undressed. He had been blown up, and every stitch of clothing had been ripped from his body. When picked up later he did not know his name or regiment.

The Commanding Officer and I toured the Battalion's new position, coming under the whisking fire of the machine-gun on our left flank. It would be necessary to deal with it. Little did we realise that, although then in the van of the fighting, we should soon be walking nonchalantly about while troops

charged up the hill a mile and a half beyond.
For these were the days of " leap frog," and
later in the morning troops came though us
with fresh and more distant objectives to
capture, and in the afternoon we hailed the
First Battalion Grenadier Guards as it
passed by in artillery formation.

We followed the progress of its men—
now spectators of, instead of participants in
a battle. First row seats and not a damned
cent to pay. On they went, over a mile or
so of country, until they reached the foot of a
ridge where, the battalion extending, the
men could be seen charging up the slope to
the hectic measure of a mass of machine-
guns.

Meanwhile, our Field Artillery came
galloping up, unlimbering and going into
action, and I thought of the early days of
1915 when we used to practise just such a
manœuvre.

7

We thought we should get a rest after this

show but we got little more than a respite, during which time " Bulgy " left us to take over a brigade and I for one felt very sorry.

Soon we were on the march—no one knew with what object—over the destroyed and dismal country of the Somme, now being wrested once more from the enemy.

At dusk the Battalion was halted for supper. We were told that it was to attack the following morning. I was doing temporary Intelligence Officer and was sent ahead to our jumping-off positions.

A black night, a hell of a long walk. I had the greatest difficulty finding the way, as did the Battalion itself, which finally turned up almost simultaneously with zero hour.

The day before, the battle had gone forward until, when we went over, our artillery was firing at extreme ranges. The result was that we got seventeen casualties from our " shorts " and none from the Boche, who had retired during the night.

We passed a trench full of dead Jocks and Germans in the grip of a last death struggle, an enemy artillery limber complete with horses and riders all killed by a single shell, and over a sunken road that stank with the dead of a German artillery wagon line. . . .

It wasn't until nightfall that we gained touch with the enemy and by the next day we were occupying with the Germans the Hindenburg line—a terrible mix-up. Gradually the Boche withdrew across the Canal du Nord.

Gas shelling began. Those sinister shells which land with a harmless, snuffed sound, like duds, but soon poison the air. The men adjusted box respirators, but a good many were too late and went away with splotched and streaming faces.

*   *

*

Chapter IX

I

It was autumn. In America the trees were turning from green into burnished browns and gold and yellow and red. The maples turn yellow. The dogwood and mulberry turn red. On the hillside they stand out— each tree a separate bouquet.

I was back again near Cambrai where I had been a year before.

We were out of the line but that meant nothing, for those were days when if there was not actual battle, battle was in the air.

A German plane came over and, flying along our line, shot down four observation balloons. I watched each one as it was hit, shrivel into a sheet of flame, while its occupants drifted down in parachutes.

Soon we were in the line again. This time south of the Bapaume-Cambrai road and close to the Canal du Nord. We were company in the front-line.

The Boche had " the wind up." During my tour of duty we were suddenly swept with a hurricane of shells. It lasted about five minutes. When it was over the trench looked as though it needed a broom. Bits of dirt, wire, shell splinters, sandbag, strewn along it everywhere. . . .

That night we were relieved by the Scots Guards. Our trench was a part of their jumping-off position. After the relief had been completed they came in for a terrific shelling and suffered considerably.

We reached a point in the communication trench at which the men of the Company were given the shelter of a big dugout, and there remained for the rest of the night. The Company was in Brigade reserve and unless needed for an emergency was not scheduled to take part in the battle.

Zero hour was at 5.20 and promptly at that minute all the guns crowding the area behind let out a prolonged blast. Those were moments when to the ear all was noise, while the mind took on a silence of another sort— the complete absence of familiar sound.

I struggled out of a very deep dugout, up the steps crowded with the men of my Company, and into the early morning air—and then all alone I stood a witness of this ever awe-inspiring, this tremendous and transfixing thing called battle. It was still dark enough for the shells to flash with a certain splendour all along the Boche line, forging the horizon into a savage furnace (there is an incendiary shell that bursts into a crowd of great sparks that is very 4th-of-Julyish, and must terrify the enemy).

The morning light appeared, faint and pallid against these flaming particles, but day transformed them into a multitude of geysers spouting smoke and dirt. Bourlon Wood, on high ground, from which there was excellent observation, entirely disappeared behind our artillery smoke screen.

And while I watched—four hours or more —there passed me by a parade no other eye may see. Battalion after battalion in battle order moved, with no martial tread, no swinging up the Champs Elysées or down

Fifth Avenue or up the Mall, but rather
with bowed heads and the patient step of
choir boys, along the little valley at my feet.
But dauntlessly, relentlessly they moved as
any stream, while battalion after battalion
disappeared over the ridge to melt into the
wide ocean of battle, to give the finishing
punch, to carry our lines forward to their
final objectives.

Soon the backwash of their advance
drifted by in the stretcher cases and walking
wounded and prisoners. Some of the men
of the company who had gathered about me
greeted good-humouredly their enemies the
Germans, treating them like children, rather
inferior children, but still children, who did
not know any better.

"Hello, Jerry! Got a souvenir?"

"Have a drink, Jerry."

The German drank and said "Gute."

The Englishman laughed delightedly and
said triumphantly, "I told you he'd say
'gut.'"

On top of this, we were suddenly changed
from spectators to participants, as an order

arrived for the Company to "mop up"
an enemy strong point that had held out
all day. It was with very different feelings
and in complete silence that we moved
off now that we were to take part in the
show. We advanced along the communication trench, glad of any slight halt or
delay that counted just that many minutes
of comparative safety. We had almost
reached our jumping-off position when a
command came to about turn. The party
of the enemy had surrendered. The officer
in command gave himself up, smoking a
cigar, wearing white gloves and carrying
a stick.

2

For a minute we were out of it—not
far out—bivouacked in that part of the
Somme which had felt the ebb and flow
of battle throughout so great a part of the
war. It presented a dismal prospect.

The Battalion had come through with

few casualties. One officer had a terrible experience. With a section (about seven men) he had been detailed to work up a trench. He encountered a small party of the enemy, who surrendered. He could not spare a man as escort and so told his prisoners to find their own way back into the British lines. After the Germans had gone around a traverse in the trench one of them whipped out a concealed hand grenade and threw it at his captors. The bomb hit the top of the parapet and exploded without doing any damage, but it might have " done in " the lot. Naturally incensed at this duplicity, the British took no more prisoners. The officer himself killed seven Germans in cold blood who tried to surrender. Some squealed like pigs. But what else could he do ? He had the lives of his own men to consider and could not run the risk of further treachery. That German who threw the bomb, instead of killing any English, was responsible for the death of some thirty odd of his own countrymen—war is certainly hell !

3

A day or two after the battle I was summoned to the Orderly Room, and handed a piece of paper. Paris leave!

With it came a realisation of the power to live, a breathless eagerness to crowd into a single week the habits, the emotions, the adventure of a lifetime.

4

The train slid smoothly into the Gare du Nord as I held the door half open to be off the moment it stopped. Sight, sound and smell of Paris are distinctive, and the combination strikes the three senses simultaneously, giving a peculiar thrill—add to that being alone and on one's own, and consider the contrast afforded by the war, and an idea may be obtained of a soldier's reaction to Paris leave.

I had a room at the Ritz overlooking the garden, and had a hot, though shallow bath. It was eight o'clock. Where should I dine?

I dined alone at Larue. As I entered I sensed

a woman. My olfactory nerves were as keen as one's palate after fasting. I felt her presence before I saw her, and picked a table opposite.

She was lovely, dark, but very fair. Her hair was short, her nose was short and her upper lip was short. In fact everything turned up, as piquant as you might wish. Her teeth were white and regular—I saw that when she laughed, which she did with artless frequency. Her lips were full and red. She was about as desirable as a woman could possibly be to a man such as I with five months' total abstinence, five months' savagery, five months' thinking behind me.

She observed me too—I could imagine her saying " Jeune officer anglais "—but then, with that perfect discretion of a French-woman, she never looked at me again. I looked at her though—enough to have annoyed her companions, another woman and two French officers. But they paid no attention. They quite understood.

They remained a long time, while I listened with pleasure to their voices rising (hers quite musically) with the animation of their talk. I envied the men with her to the point of misery.

I lingered over my coffee until she left. Did she glance in my direction? I almost believe so and yet her glance was so swift, so slightly interrogative. I wanted to follow her. My God, I might never see her again!

I summoned the maître d'hotel.

"Cette dame qui vient de partir vous la connaissez de nom?"

He spread his hands in a material blessing.

"Elle s'appelle Madame Moreau."

"Madame Moreau!" I repeated it as though I had known all along.

Paying my bill I strolled out and up the street into the Place de la Concorde, the most beautiful spot in any city. Along the Champs Elysées a mild wind troubled the trees.

All at once the long day and its variety of emotions brought its reaction and I was overcome with fatigue. Walking along the rue de Rivoli, under its arcades, I turned down and entered the Place Vendôme.

Entering my room I was very soon undressed. I sank into bed with a sensation of
delicious security, and was lost at once in
the complete oblivion of a soldier's sleep.

I woke to see the sun filtering through the
curtained window, and to the thought of
Madame Moreau. How could I meet her?

How well I felt! And how amazingly
happy. Would one week's sheer joy balance
five months of war?

I shaved and bathed and dressed while
that tune, " Till the clouds roll by " kept
running through my head.

" When the rain goes a-pitter-patter,
    And you want to be safe in bed,
    Skies are weeping,
    All the world is sleeping,
    Trouble heaping
    On your head.
    It is vain to remain and chatter,
    Or to wait for a clearer sky,
    Helter-skelter
    We will run for shelter
    Till the clouds roll by."

It would become a motif for the day, and
I would act up to it with a light but wistful
heart.

All who were on Paris leave foregathered
at the Crillon bar. What a sight it was, that
changing handful of men in the uniform of
three armies. Will I ever recapture that
atmosphere of fleeting revelry ? Of laughter
that cannot conceal a look in eyes that
smouldered like eyes in a mask ? I spent an
hour in the morning there drinking cocktails, laughing and chatting.

Herbert Haseltine arrived. He was attached to the camouflage section of the U.S.
Army. He had on a smart pair of light
coloured khaki breeches and light coloured
puttees to which, he said, his commanding
officer, a regular (West Pointer), objected.
" You look like a Gawd-damn Englishman
going out on a hunt ! "

He also carried a stick, contrary to regulations in the American Army. Every time
it was taken away from him he bought
another.

The morning after Herbert's arrival in

camp his major, up bright and early, paid him a visit.

" Is there anything you would like ? "

" Some hot water to shave with."

" Hot water-r ! I haven't used hot water for three years."

Herbert speaks French, German, Italian, Spanish and English. When the Major heard this, he said, looking at him suspiciously :

" You a linguist ? "

Willie Crocker and Will Stewart turned up. I thought Will would know Madame Moreau. He did.

" Can you fix it ? "

" I fixed it long ago ! "

" I mean can you fix it for me ? " . . .

We all lunched at Henri.

After luncheon we took a ' salon particulier ' and Cole Porter played the piano for three hours.

" When the rain goes a-pitter-patter,
    And you want to be safe in bed. . . ."

Time was slipping from me, melting away.

The afternoon passed with the speed of an hour—although I did nothing but walk through the Tuileries, wondering why the leaves fell so much sooner in Paris than in the country (in the spring they bloom earlier), and then over the Seine and along the Quai, picking up old books for the sake of indulging a peaceful pursuit.

And then a gala night ! Ten of us dined at the Café de Paris. Five Americans and five British (counting myself as British because of my uniform). Orpen was one of us. After dinner we pressed one hundred franc notes into his hands and told him to pay the bill. He expostulated that we had given him too much, but nobody seemed to care. Everyone was, if not the worse, certainly the better for drink. We had reached that stage—an ascending scale. Alfred followed a fair thing out, and was never seen again. " C.G." was suffering from shell shock—or so he maintained. (He was in hospital on the outskirts of Paris and was so shell shocked that he wandered to the Crillon bar every day, and when he had got back to hospital did not seem to be

able to tell the authorities where he had been.)
Monty was conservative—he was fighting the
battle of Paris—and doing it well ; he was the
wit of the evening.   (One day he telephoned
from the Crillon for a Ford truck and was
sent four trucks.   He entered the first and
solemnly drove around Paris stopping for
drinks on the way.)   " D " from our first
battalion had the attitude more of an
astonished and incredulous observer than a
participant in this vortex.   Healey and I
were on the crest ; I was thrilled ; here was
life and a-plenty ; the heightened atmosphere
generated by fair and adventurous women
and adventurous men—for the moment out
of danger. . . .

We went on to the Folies Bergére.   Every
officer on Paris leave was there and every
woman in Paris.   An indescribable scene.
Monty saw some women in a box he knew.
(He was practically a resident of Paris.)   One,
lo and behold, was " La Dame du Restaurant."   I was overcome.   We all went to the
house of one, the mistress of——.   C.G., by
this time almost " unconscious," sat heavily

on a chair in the hall saying resolutely, " I
won't go upstairs."

We danced to a gramophone, " Wait till
you see me with my Sweetie " and drank
champagne until early morning, when Marise
Moreau and I hand in hand skippped across
the Champs Elysées—to the thin, cool peep
of an autumn morning, buoyed by the
simple thrill of being alive. Alive! That
is all one needed for happiness those days
—just to keep being alive! Picking up a
horse fiacre, we drove in a leisurely way—
though all too quickly—through the dim
and empty streets . . .

" Marise ! "

" Ma chérie ! "

(" Wait till you see me with my Sweetie
Looking so awfully proud . . ."

. . . " Helter skelter
We will run for shelter
Till the clouds roll by . . .")

5

Clouds ! They were hiding the sun now.

The day had grown tired before its time.

I had been back about a week or two, quite dismal at getting down to soldiering again after so delicious a taste of peace. I longed for peace. Or was it that I longed for Marise?

While I had been away the Battalion had gone into battle and the Germans were driven out of a large tract of country where little villages were standing practically intact, so that when not actually in the line our billets were good. Strange things occurred. For instance, a village stood between us and the German lines, and into it we sent a patrol. The Officer in Command, a boy of nineteen, instead of meeting Germans in the houses met a number of joyous and hysterical women who rushed at him and kissed him. A little girl who went out into the street was sniped by a German and wounded in three places. She was rescued by a couple of our men and brought in, but the poor little thing died.

Poor Sergeant Wonnacott failed to "bob" once too often, and a shell blew the back of his head off the other day. I can hear him now, saying with contempt, " That man bobs, sir."

6

November the 4th, 1918. Et voilà la fin ! I was the picturesque soldier always imagined by the writers of war stories— sitting on, well, not a camp bed, but my great article of luxury, an air mattress, in a tent, and writing by the dim and romantic light of a candle. To make the setting perfect it was raining outside, and I wondered whether it would still be raining the next day. We had to be up at three and on the move by four a.m. I was looking forward to it really, and who knew, it might be the very last battle of the war. Turkey was out of it, Austria as good as out, and Germany, even if she still maintained an army more or less intact, was certainly on her last legs and more than eager for peace. Yes ! The last hour of the war had set in ; the barrage was kicking up the mighty dust of final

193

battle, and the machine-gun ticking out its passing seconds.

"This is going to be my last battle." It was Geoffrey Gunther who spoke.

"It's going to be the last battle," I replied, looking up.

"Well, it's going to be my last battle anyway; I'm sick of the war."

"Yes, I agree. Mine too. We'll simply refuse to fight any more."

But I did not like that word "last." It stuck. It made me apprehensive.

The mail arrived with cigarettes for me. Thank God! I had run out. The prospect of a battle does two things, and one is that it makes you want to smoke. I settled down for the night. But it's so difficult to sleep with a battle on your mind.

I was wide awake and somehow re-freshed at 3.30 a.m. It had stopped raining. At four o'clock the men had their breakfasts. At 4.30 they "fell in." It was still dark. I felt I ought to say something to them.

It seems to me to-day I would like to have said, addressing that vast army of

non-combatants who were so vigorously
prosecuting the war, and quoting Wilfred
Owen :

". . . These men are worth your tears,
  You are not worth their merriment."

But in reality I said :
  " We may not meet the enemy to-day.
They may have retired."   I felt like adding,
" I hope they have."
  Still we had a big objective—Maubeuge
—some five miles away. The 3rd Battalion
constituted the second wave of the attack,
and we were due to go through the 1st
Coldstream. We (No. 1 Company) were to
be the right flank advance company. We
had a long march to our jumping-off
positions, which we were scheduled to reach
about 9 a.m. We were delayed several
times ; once, fording a stream at a point
where the bridge had been blown up by the
enemy. It took some time to get the men
across ; we were gas-shelled, and had to put
on box-respirators. The men took on the

semblance of terrified gollywogs. We
passed through a village and finally reached
our jumping-off positions—a little late I
think. We were screened by a wood. The
two front companies got into diamond
formation. The day was fine and cold. We
started off through the wood, No. 2 Company on our left. The Germans were shelling
the wood and a shell struck a tree on our
immediate right with a mighty crash—like a
giant axe splitting it at a stroke. Clouds of
shrapnel bursting high scudded before the
wind as though the elements were bent on
minimising their effect. The men moved
forward with heads slightly bowed, like
people going through a heavy downpour.

Passing through the wood without
casualties, we came upon two Germans who
had escaped being " mopped up " by the
Coldstream. One was sitting up. Some
of the men fired, but he did not change his
position. When we reached him we found
he was dead, propped up in a shallow trench.
The other ran and although fired at, got
away. We continued to advance until we

reached a ridge, what the map would call a contour. From this elevation the ground fell away to a road, about a thousand yards off, running along our front. From the road the ground rose again to a ridge opposite, perhaps three thousand yards from where we stood. Quarter right and on the road itself lay a group of three or four houses—a big farm.

For a few seconds I noticed the country spread before me, and then we came under heavy machine-gun fire. I withdrew the men behind the ridge until the bullets whipped overhead. Allan Adair came up on our left, and we discussed the situation. We decided the houses on my right front were occupied by the enemy and concealed machine-guns. I determined to attack them, half the men advancing in short rushes while the other half covered their advance with rifle fire. We started out, but came again under so heavy a fire that a half dozen men were hit at once. Both the men on either side of me fell wounded—one was Corporal Clark, the smartest soldier I have seen. I realised that at this rate we could soon be wiped out, and so retired again to comparative safety behind the ridge. The experience of having one's men hit and hearing their groans and being responsible for it turned me sick for a moment. The instinctive antidote was action, and I decided to attack the houses from a flank, making a detour to our right and taking advantage of every rise in the ground.

When about a hundred yards from the houses we rushed them. I shouted to the men to scatter into the different houses and dashed into one, revolver in hand. Not a German was found. Either they had seen us and retired, or else they had never occupied the houses but had been firing at us from other " hidden machine-gun nests." Rather relieved, we lined the road. The main thing was to advance, whether we met Germans or not, and that we were doing.

From the road a narrow cart track led to high ground on our front ; otherwise, fields with hedges so thick you could not force a way through them, bounded the road.

While I was considering the best method of advancing, the enemy began shelling the road. One shell knocked out five or six men, a tiny splinter going into my note-book, and rather than run the risk of more casualties while we cut a way through a hedge with a billhook (which would have taken time) I led the men up the cart track. I was afraid of coming under point-blank machine-gun fire, which, down this narrow way, would have meant slaughter. We passed the wreck of a German field gun on our left, and three-fourths of the way up the hill a field spread out on our left and right. I ordered the men to extend, and continuing to advance, came again under machine-gun fire. Profiting by my lesson, I at once ordered the men to right turn. We cut our way through a hedge, and, starting to semi-circle, came across poor Gunther with the other half of the Company. He was in very good form. He pointed to a house—" I think there are Germans in there ! Shall I attack it and get a V.C. ? "

" No," I answered. (He was to deserve a

V.C. later !) We parted and I went on.
We came across an empty trench, and
finally to another field. Here we found a
gap in the hedge. We went through and
found ourselves at once under direct machine
gun fire two hundred yards from our left
front. We could see the Germans and
opened fire with rifles and Lewis gun.

Meanwhile I thought to attack it at the
same time from a flank, and leading a
detachment to my left started along the
hedge. I had hardly run twenty yards,
however, when I was hit and fell forward
into the beginning of a trench a foot deep.
Here I lay for perhaps an hour. The
pain was in the right hip. Gunther ran
out to me. As I looked round he fell
and I saw the rip at the back of his jacket
where the bullet had gone out. He died
almost at once. A private soldier shot
through both arms fell at the same time, and
together we lay until the battle had gone on
ahead and stretcher bearers turned up. I
was in too much pain to be picked up, and
dragged myself on to the stretcher. Carried

back, I passed the M.O. A field dressing having been put on the wound, I passed No. 3 Company and soon after reached Battalion Headquarters. The Commanding Officer, Lord Lascelles, threw himself down beside me as they placed the stretcher on the ground and to my surprise seemed much moved. I said I was cold and he covered me with his British warm.

When they picked me up the perfect Battalion Sergeant-major said, "Leave the Commanding Officer's coat." I was carried a mile or two over broken country by two medical corps men and two German prisoners. It seemed we would never reach the end of our journey. Every step was a jolt and every jolt intense pain. We reached a field which looked like a battlefield, so many wounded lay about—British and Germans. I heard someone say, " That house is mined " which explained our being put down in a field. It was now late in the afternoon. I was so cold that my fingers stuck out stiff and numb and I couldn't move them. I had milk chocolate in my pocket and gave it away. It

was dusk when a horse ambulance picked me
up. The bridges blown up, horse ambulances
were being used to ford the stream.

We reached the Advanced Field Dressing
Station, a large farm. It was dark. I was
put down in a courtyard, while a Padre
said, "Anyone want any tea? If you've
been shot in the stomach, don't drink it as it
will kill you."

I drank five cups of tea and felt revived.
I was carried into a room and put on a table.
My breeches were cut away and I gave away
my boots—they were good ones. I was
properly bandaged. I asked if my wound
was serious, and was told no. After a bit I
was put in a motor ambulance and taken to
the Rear Field Dressing Station. One of the
others in the ambulance was Corporal Clark.
At the Dressing Station I was given an
injection of anti-tetanus. The Medical
Officer who gave it, recognised me. He had
been attached to the Third Battalion on the
Somme in 1916. From the Dressing Station
to the Casualty Clearing Station was a long
drive. It began to rain as we left and

continued all night. It was perhaps 7 or 8 p.m. when we started out and it was about 5 a.m. when we reached the Casualty Clearing Station. The driver had lost his way. All night we slushed along the road. One wounded occupant who was suffering terribly groaned ceaselessly.

The Casualty Clearing Station at Cambrai was overflowing. There was no empty cot in the officers' ward, and I was put in a private soldiers' ward in which every other cot was occupied. Later in the morning I was examined by a Medical Officer, an Australian, who assured me the bullet had hit nothing vital. I was then put in the officers' ward, and as there was still no empty cot, left on the stretcher. At night I had the fear that I would be stepped on by mistake. An officer next to me, badly wounded in the face, suffered in silence. The rest of the day and that night was spent in the Casualty Clearing Station and the following morning I was one of those placed in a crowded Red Cross train, new and British-built, berths in three tiers on either side of each car and every berth occupied. By this time I was in agony. I was given an injection of morphia which eased the pain and relaxed every nerve and muscle. Our destination was Rouen, which we reached after a journey of a day and a night. From the station I was brought to No. 8 (General) Hospital, a building originally a monastery, which had been a German Hospital in the war of 1870. Two years before I had been there, " sick."

For days these lines went through my head, in my sleep and in my delirium, over and over and over, an endless refrain :

" Give to these children new to the world,
　　Rest far from men.
Is anything better, anything better—
　　Tell us it then :
Us who are old, old and gay—
　　O so old,
Thousands of years, thousands of years,
　　If all were told."

One line from another poem would follow : " For the world's more full of weeping than you can understand."

204

Epilogue

No. 8 (General) Hospital
    Rouen.

Feb. 23, 1919.

DEAR FATHER—

The cold is so great that I can emerge from seven blankets only long enough to put down that things seem to be going fairly well.

The prospects of coming to England soon are good. I ought to make it by March. We are four "femurs" left. The other three are fit to travel—I am keeping them waiting. My wound is still discharging. To-night they changed my tubes—put in smaller ones. It hurt some. I jumped a yard in the air—never thought I could have done it—and the orderly nearly dropped me !

My one excitement is food from the Hotel

de la Poste which a little chasseur brings up twice a week. (The Hospital chickens are served with their feathers still on!) Also, since your visit, special dishes occasionally arrive from the Restaurant de la Cathédrale brought by Madame herself, who sits and entertains me for a while.

I never told you, did I, that the men must have thought I was killed, for I got a letter intended for you from my servant in which he began, " We were all so sorry about your son's death, etc." I meant to forward it to you, but I lost it.

I get moments of discouragement—it's slow—too slow. I suddenly get a temperature of 101 after days of fairly normal. This cold has effected my feet in a curious way—they get boiling hot at night and I have to leave them out naked—even then they remain just as hot and drive me nearly crazy.

I can see myself a querulous, cranky invalid all my life. I can see it. People will be bored by it, for they will have forgotten the war. Some of the nurses here

have already. The night superintendent
doesn't yet know there has been one. You
should have heard her berate an officer
because he was having a hemorrhage. The
night I had an abscess in my wound she
gave me the devil. " Do you want me to
disturb your surgeon ? "

" No, I want some morphia."

" Haven't you had aspirin ? "

" It hasn't done any good."

" Well, that's all you'll get. I suppose
you're going to keep the ward awake all
night."

I was glad to see her go after that.

The officers all hate her. One evening
when she arrived they let out cat-calls and
boo'ed. She said, " I thought you were
officers and gentlemen, but I see I'm in a
stable." Everyone laughed. It was strange
to watch them, these trapped, these swathed
and prostrate marionettes, arms and legs at
acute angles outstretched in splints hoisted
with ropes that run through pulleys fastened
to the ceiling, on the ends of which sand-
bags dangle. It was grotesque to watch

them in this inquisition of weird and painful, of cruel and impossible positions, their beds shaking with their hysterical laughter.

It's a weary world and the raspberry jam sent me from Paris is all finished now. . . .

*   *

*

Appendix

A STORY OF THE GRENADIER GUARDS

THE origin of the Regiment dates from Flanders, where, during the exile of Charles II, it was created in 1656 as His Majesty's Royal Regiment of Guards. Its nucleus was 400 staunch Royalists who, following Charles, flocked to his standard as soon as it was learned that an alliance with Spain had been concluded whereby it was agreed to raise a British force on the continent. Most of those who joined had served against Cromwell and they were forced to accept lower ranks than they had previously held but " all were very willing to submit to such a state of things."

The Regiment began its history in the spirit in which it was continued, when it received its baptism of fire at the battle of the Dunes near Dunkirk in 1658. Its allies the Spaniards behaved much as they did many years later at Barossa and quitted the

field with undue acceleration, leaving the
Guards " alone and unsupported . . . determined to maintain their honour . . .
and the cause of their lawful sovereign."
(One officer in Bristol's Irish Regiment,
which had also retired, joined them, a
certain Captain Strode. After the fight he
was taken into the Regiment and 28 years
later he died as its commanding officer.)
Meanwhile the French and Cromwell's men
had passed the little party on either side and
the second line of the French had come up
under the command of the Marquis de
Rambures " who having much esteem for
Charles II and observing this small body of
men . . . deserted by their allies . . . went
up . . . to offer them quarter. They replied that they had been posted there by the
duke and were therefore resolved to maintain that ground as long as they were able."
De Rambures said, in effect, that it would
be foolish for them to hold out as their entire
army had retreated, and to prove it he
conducted two officers to a hill where they
were able to see for themselves the truth of

his statement. They then agreed to surrender but only on their own terms, namely, that " they should not be delivered up to the English, nor be stripped, nor have their pockets searched." De Rambures agreed to this " giving his word for its due performance . . . and the promise was scrupulously kept . . ."

Many people are still under the impression that the Foot Guards are kept at home to do sentry duty outside of the Royal Palaces.

Major Aubrey-Fletcher in his foreword to " A History of the Foot Guards " tells how before the Great War, a lady, next to whom he was sitting at dinner, announced that " The Guards looked very nice . . . it was a pity they didn't fight." Even the Great War did not kill this strange illusion, for at Arras in December, 1917, " just after the Guards Division had finished a three months' engagement at Paschendaele, followed by a terrible ordeal at Fontaine-Notre-Dame, and culminating in the great counter-attack at Gouzeaucourt which alone saved the British Army from a disastrous defeat, an entry appeared in the Suggestion Book of the Officers' Club, asking "when the 'Guardees' were going to do some fighting." It was in 1918 that Pryce with his handful of men, who had refused to surrender and were slaughtered to the last man, held in check several battalions of the enemy for two days and two nights while the Australians came up, detrained and took up positions in their rear. One might almost say, with some exaggeration, that Pryce saved the Channel ports ! It is no exaggeration to say that a Guards Brigade may have done so. That kind of thing is not mentioned in despatches.

What is the reason for this idea, this superstition that the Brigade of Guards does no fighting ? The power of suggestion ? The word " Guards " brings to mind the scarlet tunic and bear-skin of the sentry outside of Buckingham Palace. He is there and has been there year in year out (if not Buckingham Palace some other Royal Palace) in war time as in peace time. It is thus he is visualized at the mention of the word " Guards." Another reason may be the

212

fact that military historians rarely specifically mention regiments. Even in Napier's account of Barossa, where the 2nd Battalion First Guards, some 600 strong, lost one out of every three engaged, the Foot Guards are not named. Whatever the reason, the fact that the Grenadier Guards have some twenty-four battle honours and have figured in most wars, speaks for itself.

Permit this Guardsman, therefore, to be taken from his sentry box and presented in a series of " lantern slides " which show a different background.

Steenkirk, 1692 ! The 2nd Battalion First Guards was one of several battalions to attack at dawn a position held by nearly five times their number. The French position was taken and when the small force which had remained unsupported was finally driven back by vastly superior numbers the First Guards left half its strength upon the field.

At Landen, 1693, a Guards Brigade with some Hanoverians held Neerwinder, the key to the position, occupied by William of

Orange. Among others was the 1st Battalion First Guards. In trenches east of the village was the 2nd Battalion First Guards. Twice driven out, the defenders of Neerwinder twice recovered their position against greatly superior numbers. Only the third attempt dislodged them, and with this assault completed half the First Guards lay dead and wounded on the field.

At Blenheim the First Guards took part in the bloody attack on that village, at which point in the battle the British were out-numbered five to one. Thirty paces from the palisade they were met by a murderous fire which " struck down many a gallant fellow." The remainder pressing on, " attempted by sheer strength to drag away the palings ; they fired through the intervals or struck at the Frenchmen with swords and muskets. Dormer, commanding the battalion, was killed ; Mordaunt lost an arm, and young Campion was desperately wounded in the nearly successful attempt to pull away the wooden barrier . . ."

During the War of Independence, a

composite battalion of Foot Guards number-
ing 1,000 strong was sent to America.
Thirteen officers in the First Guards were
included and 465 other ranks. (Four officers
came from the 3rd Battalion.) "They
were ordered to supply themselves with a
uniform with white lace, and to discontinue
carrying spontoons and halberts . . . a report being current that the Americans were
in the habit of picking off the officers." The
King reviewed the Battalion March 19, 1776,
on Wimbledon Common on the eve of its
departure. In New York "the equestrian
statue of George III was pulled down by
rebels, to the great indignation of the Guards
at such an insult being offered to their
Sovereign." The Guards figured in the
battles of White Plains, Brandywine, German-
town and Guilford Court House (where
they had four officers killed and seven
wounded). Lord Cornwallis in his despatch
said, "The gallantry of General O'Hara
merits my highest commendation, for after
receiving two dangerous wounds he continued on the field while the action lasted,

and by his earnest attention . . . seconded
. . . his Majesty's Guards, who are no less
distinguished by their order and discipline
than by their spirit and valour." Among
officers taken prisoner by the Americans
was a certain Captain Asgill of the First
Guards, who "had only come out to
America in the spring of 1781. In con-
sequence of the . . . execution of Captain
Huddy, an American officer, in the spring of
1782, the life of one of the British officers,
then prisoners of war, was demanded in
retaliation. One officer from each regiment
was first selected, and on drawing lots . . .
the chance fell upon Captain Asgill, who on
the 27th of May was closely imprisoned,
removed from Lancaster to Chatham, loaded
with chains and threatened with death. A
gallows of unusual height was erected
in sight of his prison window placarded
with these words : 'For the execution of
Captain Asgill.' He continued in confinement till the 13th of November, 1782, when
he was released by the authority of the
American Congress, as explained in a letter

addressed to him by General Washington.

'Head Quarters, Nov. 13th, 1782.
'It affords me singular pleasure to have it
in my power to transmit you the enclosed
copy of an Act of Congress of the 7th inst.
by which you are released from the disagreeable circumstances in which you have so
long been. Supposing you would wish to
go into New York as soon as possible, I
enclose a passport for that purpose.
'Your letter of the 18th of October came
regularly to my hands. I beg you to believe
that my not answering it sooner did not
proceed from inattention to you, or a want of
feeling for your situation. I daily expected
a determination in your case, and I thought it
better to await that, than to feed you with
hopes that might in the end prove fruitless.
You will attribute my detention of the
enclosed letter, which has been in my hands
about a fortnight, to the same cause.
'I cannot take leave of you, sir, without
assuring you that in whatever light my
agency in this unpleasing affair may be

217

received, I never was influenced through the whole of it by sanguinary motives, but by what I conceived a sense of my duty, which loudly called upon me to take measures, however disagreeable, to prevent a repetition of those enormities which have been the subject of discussion; and that this important end is likely to be answered without the effusion of the blood of an innocent person is not a greater relief to you, than it is to, sir,

'Your most obedient,

'And humble servant,

'G. WASHINGTON.'

"Captain Asgill at once made his way to New York, and returned by the earliest opportunity to England." It is nice to know that after this narrow escape Charles Asgill lived to become a General in 1814.

In the Peninsular, in 1809, under Sir John Moore, during the harassing retreat (250 miles) to Coruña, "The corps in which there was the least straggling were the artillery, the Guards and the reserve. The Guards were the strongest body of men in the army and consequently suffered least from fatigue ; besides, they are strictly disciplined . . ."

As the retreating army entered Coruña Sir John Moore himself said, " Arbuthnot, look at that body of men in the distance ; they are the Guards by the way they are marching." They were ! They marched into Coruña at the end of their 250 miles " with drums beating, the drum major in front flourishing his stick . . . drill sergeants on the flanks keeping the men in step, exactly as if they were on their own drill ground at home." (Plus ça change, plus c'est la même chose !)

At Barossa the Spaniards with astonishing speed left the field *and* the British in a situation fraught with difficulty and possible disaster. Out-numbered two to one, they ran the risk, if they retreated, of being badly cut up in the narrow peninsula. General Graham, on a magnificent impulse, a desperate chance or the genius of true generalship, ordered his numerically inferior battalions to attack. Riding forward and waving his hat, he cried, " Now my lads, there they are, spare your powder, but give them steel enough." Dilkes at the head of the 2nd Battalion First Guards advanced rapidly against the French—as he himself rather naïvely put it, "I may say with distinguished gallantry." His men crossed a deep hollow, under a heavy fire. They came up in loose order but " in a fighting mood " . . . " Their gallant opponents met them " . . . Ruffin fell. . . . Sebright was carried off the field wounded. Dilkes had his horse killed under him. It was a bloody fight and the Foot Guards alone lost 219 out of 600, but they drove the French from the battlefield while La Peña with his Spaniards looked amiably on. . . .

Fortescue writes that at Quatre Bras " The Guards also maintained worthily their high reputation, being thrown into action at a very trying moment after a march of 26 miles, with shaken troops on every side of them." Their casualties were heavy. " In the First Guards, the 2nd and 3rd Battalions lost over five hundred out of two thousand rank and file."

At Waterloo Maitland's and Byng's bri-
gades of Guards occupied a hill behind
Hougoumont, and it consequently devolved
chiefly upon them to defend this key
position. Defend it they did, until 8,000
Frenchmen had fallen in a gallant but vain
endeavour to drive them back.

It was at the very last that Napoleon
played his trump card, and his Imperial
Guard, in two dense columns, with a frontage of about 80 men and a depth of some
nine ranks, " with five generals at their head
and Ney in front of all," began to move
against the Allies. The 3rd and 4th Battalions were the first to come into action
and it was against the 3rd Battalion First
Guards that their attack developed. " As
the French . . . approached the crest, they
could see no enemy before them, but when
within thirty yards of the sunken road a
voice rang out above the din of battle,
' Stand up, Guards,' and out of the very
ground before them rose a solid wall of
scarlet tipped with steel." The red-coats
poured volley after volley into the mass of

advancing Frenchmen. " So close were the
enemy that the front file of Guards were
firing from the hip. . . . Gradually the
great column began to crumble, till, at a word
from Wellington, Maitland gave the order
and the First Guards, dashing forward with
the bayonet, swept their redoubtable ad-
versaries headlong down the slope. . . .
The defeat of the Guard had an instantaneous
effect upon the whole French army. ' La
Garde recule ! ' "

During the battle Wellington was overheard to say, " Guards, you shall be re-
warded for this." And they were. " In
1815 the Prince Regent was pleased to
approve of the First Regiment of Foot
Guards being styled ' The First or Grenadier
Regiment of Foot Guards ' in commemora-
tion of their having defeated the Grenadiers
of the French Imperial Guard at Waterloo."

At Alma the Grenadiers " with their tall
caps " were to be seen " advancing . . . firm
as a wall in their discipline and regularity."
Lieutenant Burgoyne, carrying the Colour,
being shot in the ankle, the Colour was

seized by Lieutenant B. W. Hamilton, who was hit by a spent ball but continued to carry the Colour throughout the attack. The battalion later becoming isolated, stood "firm as a rock, pouring in its fire to the front, and to the left unsupported for a time on either flank."

"C'était trop majestueux," commented the French after the battle.

After Inkerman a French officer, addressing a Guardsman, with traditional courtesy, and I hope sincerity, observed, "A présent je comprends Waterloo." (Shade of Monsieur de Rambures! One can almost imagine it is he who is speaking.)

*   *

*

CHAPTER NOTES

CHAPTER NOTES

Chapter I (pp. 7–21)
pp. 13–18 The "impromptu corps" was the Intelligence Corps, formed 5th August 1914, when telegrams were dispatched to unsuspecting men in all walks of life, asking them to join the new Corps. "All had been previously earmarked, and all had one thing in common, they were either linguists or experts in some aspect of European life". In its early days the Corps was commanded by Major T. G. Torrie and the Adutant was Captain J. A. Dunnington-Jefferson. See: Lt.-Col. B.A.H. Parritt, *The Intelligencers* (N.p., n.d.), p. 232.
p. 18 2/Lt. Julian Martin Smith, Intelligence Corps, died of wounds, 10th October 1914.

Chapter II (pp. 22–34)
p. 22 The Bentinck Hotel was at 17 and 18 Margaret Street.

p. 22 Peter Donne remains unidentified.

p. 27 Lt. O. D. Filley. R.F.C.

p. 28 2/Lt. N. H. Read, R.F.C.

p. 28 Lt. Dillwyn Parrish Starr, 2/Coldstream Guards, killed in action, 16th September 1916. Born in Philadelphia in 1884 and educated at Harvard. After working with the French as a volunteer ambulance driver he joined the Royal Naval Armoured Car Division and served with them in France and Gallipoli. He was gazetted a Temporary Sub-Lieutenant in the Royal Naval Volunteer Reserve in May 1915 and, at the suggestion of Walter Oakman, transferred to the Coldstream Guards on 10th January 1916. After his death his father produced a small memorial volume, *The War Story of Dillwyn Parrish Starr*.

p. 28 Lt. W. G. Oakman, D.S.O., Coldstream Guards. Transferred from the R.N.V.R. on 14th October 1915.

p. 28 2/Lt. A. Whitridge, Royal Artillery.

Chapter III (p. 35–50)

p. 38 Lt. Arthur Everard Hale Barton, Royal Artillery, D/50 Bde., killed in action, 25th September 1915. According to the Brigade War Diary they were keeping up a slow fire on

Haisnes Trench "but as no information as to the progress of the infantry was obtainable, at 8 am 2/Lt. [sic] A. E. Barton with two telephonists was sent forward to pick up what information he could. He and one of his telephonists were killed whilst laying out their line". (PRO: WO95/1751).

p. 40 On the 30th September the 9th Division, less the 50th Artillery Brigade, started to move north to the Ypres Salient. The 50th Brigade was not relieved until 2nd October when three of its batteries handed over their guns to the 36th Artillery Brigade (2nd Division), took over the Meerut Division's guns ("old pieces ... wobbling in every joint and gear") and set out from Cuinchy to trek north on 3rd October.

pp. 42–49 The 9th Division relieved the 17th Division near Hill 60 on 5th October 1915. It remained in the Salient until May 1916.

p. 50 Carstairs was gazetted as transferred to the Grenadier Guards as a 2/Lt. of the Special Reserve of Officers Supplementary to Regular Units or Corps on 15th November 1915.

Chapter IV (pp. 51–71)
p. 51 When Carstairs joined the 5th (Reserve) Battalion it was commanded by Lt.-Col. G. D.

White and the Adjutant was Capt. The Hon. L. P. Cary. In February 1916 Lt.-Col. White was succeeded by Lt.-Col. G. C. Hamilton, D.S.O.

p. 53 Ciro's Club was in Orange Street, near Leicester Square.

pp. 59–60 According to the regimental history the casualties of the 3/Grenadier Guards on 15th September 1916 were 17 officers and 395 other ranks killed and wounded.

p. 61 The Guards Divisional Base Depot was established at Harfleur in August 1915 and was commanded by Major A. H. Royds, Scots Guards, from 21st August 1915 to November 1918.

p. 63 According to the battalion War Diary Carstairs actually joined the battalion on 26th September 1916.

p. 65 The battalion took over from the 1/Scots Guards on 28th September just north of Lesboefs.

p. 66 Major A. F. A. N. Thorne took command of the battalion on 18th September 1916. See also notes to p. 80, below.

p. 66 Heucourt Chateau.

p. 66 For Dillwyn Starr and Walter Oakman, see notes to p. 28, above.

CHAPTER NOTES

p. 69 In 1916 the Four Hundred Club was at 6, 7 and 8 Old Bond Street.

Chapter V (pp. 72–96)
pp. 72–73 See notes to p. 61, above.
p. 73 The 7th (Guards) Entrenching Battalion was formed in November 1915 and remained in existence until September 1917 when it was the last such battalion to be disbanded. It reappeared the following month as a Reinforcement Battalion and in due course it had its name changed to the Guards Works Battalion. It was reduced to cadre in April 1918.

p. 75 Capt. (A/Major) E. C. Ellice, D.S.O., Grenadier Guards. His son was 2/Lt. A. R. Ellice, Grenadier Guards, died of wounds, 29th September 1916.

p. 80 Lt.-Col. A. F. A. N. Thorne, D.S.O. [Gen. Sir A. F. A. N. Thorne, K.C.B., C.M.G., D.S.O. 1885–1970].

p. 80 Major G. E. C. Rasch, D.S.O. [Br. G.E.C. Rasch, C. V. O., D.S.O. 1885–1955].

pp. 83–84 The battalion sustained 40 casualties from bombing between 4th September and 11th September 1917.

p. 87 Sgt. Thomas James Wonnacott, D.C.M.,

killed in action, 4th November 1918. See also
p. 192.
p. 91 Capt. J. C. Craigie, M.C.; Lt. The Hon.
H. E. Eaton.

Chapter VI (pp. 97–117)
p. 106 Lt. A. C. Knollys, M. C.
p. 109 The battalion was relieved by 1/Essex
(88th Bde., 29th Div.) during the night of
21st/22nd September 1917.
p. 111 Major William Orpen, Official War Artist. [Major Sir William Orpen, R.A., K.B.E.
1878–1931].
p. 115–116 It would appear that only three officer casualties were sustained by the battalion
in early October 1917: Lt. J. C. D. Tetley,
killed in action, 9th October; Lt. F. W. R.
Greenhill, Intelligence Officer, killed in action,
10th October; 2/Lt. W. H. S. Roper, died of
wounds, 11th October.
p. 116 The inspection by the Duke of Connaught took place on 21st October 1917.

Chapter VII (pp. 118–143)
p. 118 Carstairs rejoined the battalion at
Hernicourt on 15th November 1917.
p. 119–123 Boulencourt appears to be a mis-

spelling for Beaulencourt which the battalion reached on 21st November 1917. They reached Lebucquiere on the 23rd, entered the newly captured trenches of the Hindenburg Support line at Ribecourt on the 24th and during the night of the 26th took over the line round the south east edge of Bourlon Wood.

p. 124 Lt. Gavin Patrick Bowes-Lyon, commanding No. 1 Co., killed in action 27th November 1917; Capt. J. S. Hughes, M.C., commanding No. 4 Co.

p. 125 2/Lt. C. W. Carrington. See p. 145 re. award of D.S.O.

p. 125 2/Lt. Sir John Ludlow Hanham.

p. 125 Capt. W. H. Beaumont-Nesbit, M.C., commanding No. 2 Co., killed in action 27th November 1917.

p. 126 Sgt. J. H. Rhodes, V. C., D.C.M. and clasp, died of wounds, 27th November 1917.

p. 130 A fellow officer's story regarding Carstairs and the advance down the main street of Fontaine-Notre-Dame is retold by Orpen in his *An Onlooker in France 1917–1919*, (London, Williams and Norgate, 1924; 2nd edn., rev.), p. 62: "Carroll was with a brother officer, and said suddenly, 'Look at the shape of that church now! Isn't it magnificent?' Another shell shrieked and hit the structure, and he said 'Damn! the fools have spoilt it!'".

p. 137 Lt. E. R. D. Hoare.

p. 139 The battalion's casualties for 27th November 1917 were 3 officers killed and 6 wounded and 270 other ranks killed and wounded.

pp. 141–143 From internal evidence it is clear that the "Kimberly" to whom Carstairs refers was an officer of the 10/Argyll and Sutherland Highlanders, the battalion that provided Ian Hay with the material for *The First Hundred Thousand* (1915) and *Carrying On – After The First Hundred Thousand* (1917). No officer named Kimberly is listed in the battalion history as having served with the 10/Argyll and Sutherland Highlanders and the most likely officer to have been hidden beneath the pseudonym is Capt. Edward William Bonnyman, D.S.O., M.C., died of wounds, 11th August 1918. See: Lt.-Col. Herbert G. Sotheby, *The 10th Battalion Argyll and Sutherland Highlanders 1914–1919*, (London, John Murray for Private Circulation, 1931), that is dedicated to the memory of Capt. Bonnyman.

Chapter VIII (pp. 144–176)

p. 145 American Medical Officer: Lt. H. C. Fish, wounded, 27th March 1918.

p. 146 Br.-Gen. C. R. Champion de Crespigny, D.S.O., commanding 1st Guards Bde., 22nd September 1917 – 18th March 1919. [Br.-Gen. Sir C. R. Champion de Crespigny, C.B., C.M.G., D.S.O. 1878–1941].

p. 146 Capt. G. H. T. Paton, V.C., M.C., killed in action, 1st December 1917. The other two officer V.Cs. were Lt.-Col. Viscount Gort, V.C., D.S.O., M.V.O., M.C., 1/Grenadier Guards and Capt. T. T. Pryce, V.C., M.C., 4/Grenadier Guards, killed in action, 13th April 1918. Regarding the latter see pp. 159–161.

p. 148 The battalion went into the line near Fampoux from 2nd to 4th January 1918.

p. 149 Capt. the Hon. A. G. Agar-Robartes, M.C.

p. 150 Carstairs' M.C. was noted in the battalion War Diary on 10th December 1917 and gazetted on 18th February 1918.

p. 151 Lady Ridley's Hospital for Wounded Soldiers was at No. 10 Carlton House Terrace.

p. 151 2/Lt. W. G. Horton, M.C., 1/Scots Guards, wounded, 27th November 1917.

"Horton ('B' Company) ... brought about a dozen men to safety from an exposed position and also carried a Lewis gun up to a position on the left and placed it there, being wounded in both wrists whilst doing so". F. Loraine Petre and others, *The Scots Guards in the Great War 1914–1918*, (London, Murray, 1925), p. 231.

p. 159 Lt. G. R. Westmacott, D.S.O., 1/Grenadier Guards, wounded, 13th March 1915.

pp. 159–161 Capt. T. T. Pryce, V.C., M.C., See note to p. 146, above.

pp. 164–165 Between 5th and 10th August 1918 elements of the 320th Regt. (160th Inf. Bde., 80th "Blue Ridge" Div., A.E.F.) were attached to the battalion.

p. 165 John Singer Sargent, R.A. (1856–1925). Official War Artist.

p. 169 2/Lt. A. D. Cooper. [Alfred Duff Cooper, 1st Viscount Norwich, P.C., G.C.M.G., D.S.O. (1890–1954)]. See his autobiography, *Old Men Forget*, (London, Hart-Davis, 1953), pp. 82–87, for an account of the period 20th–28th August 1918 during which he gained the D.S.O.

p. 175 Lt.-Col. Thorne left the battalion on

31st August 1918 to take up command of the
IX Corps School. The new Commanding Officer was Major Viscount Lascelles.

Chapter IX (pp. 177–204)
p. 183 Carstairs went on leave to Paris with
Duff Cooper on 6th October 1918. Cooper later
wrote: "I could not have chosen a better com-
panion. He knew the town as well as, or better
than, I did . . . We had many tastes in common,
including literature, cards and chess". (*Old
Men Forget*, pp. 90–91 and see also Lady Diana
Cooper, *The Rainbow Comes and Goes*, (London. Hart-Davis, 1958), pp. 208–209). Cooper
and Carstairs remained firm friends after the
war and when Cooper visited New York during
prohibition "Carstairs took me to his club,
where he not only made me a member but also
presented me with the key of his locker, well
stocked with spirits, to which he begged me
to help myself whenever I felt in need of
refreshment". (*Old Men Forget*, p. 120).
p. 187 Herbert Haseltine (1877–1962). An
American sculptor specialising in equine and
other animal subjects. His bronze group, *Les
Revenants* (Returning Spectres), representing
wounded, gassed and worn-out horses return-

ing from the front can be seen at the Imperial War Museum. An exhibition of his work was held at Knoedler's London Gallery in 1930.

p. 192 Sgt. T. J. Wonnacott. See note to p. 87, above.

p. 194 2/Lt. Geoffrey Robert Gunther, M.C., killed in action, 4th November 1918.

pp. 194–201 These extracts from the revised post-action report included in the battalion War Diary for 4th November 1918 provide a terse and vivid picture of Carstairs' last day of the war:

0300 hrs. Breakfast

0420 hrs. Battalion moved off. Approach march was hampered by the crowded state and bad condition of the roads. Lewis Guns [Limbers] had to be man-handled at places.

0600 hrs. Bridge at Villers-Pol was found to be demolished. Lewis Guns Limbers were sent up to Q.3.c, 8.5. Battalion crossed by a single plank. The crossing was shelled and one man wounded.

0800 hrs. Assembly position reached.

0830 hrs. Leading Coys. came under fire from M.G.'s. and Field Guns at close range.

0845 hrs. Leading Coys. passed through 2/C.G., who were 200 yds. short of the Green

Line on the 2nd Guards Brigade front, and captured the Green Line. No. 2 Coy. taking four 77 mm. guns and four 4.2 hows.

0920 hrs. Touch was obtained with 2/G.G. and strong patrols were pushed forward across the Aunelle River.

1000 hrs. Leading Coys. pushed forward across the Aunelle River through the orchards, the heights beyond being still in the hands of the enemy, and established themselves on the line M.4.a.8.5: M.4.d.5.3. when they came under heavy M.G. fire from the line of trenches 300 to 500 yards in front. B.H.Q., Support and Reserve Coys. moved to Sunken Road M.3.b. and d. The left flank of the battalion was now found to be completely in the air. The right flank was in touch with the 62nd Divn. The Commdg. Officer decided to push up No. 3 Coy. to protect the left flank. At the same time "C" Coy. 1/S.G. was placed at his disposal and kept in reserve.

1500 hrs. Right Coy. had worked round the enemy position and attacked it with [a] smoke grenade barrage. The enemy evacuated and they [Right Coy.] occupied the position. Lt. C. C. Carstairs, M.C. wounded and 2/Lt. G. R. Gunther killed in this operation.

1700 hrs. The left Coy. now advanced capturing Preux-au-Sart together with some prisoners and dug in on a line E. of village. This enabled the Right Coy. to advance to a line of enemy trenches 300 yds. W. of the Gommegnies – Preux-au-Sart Road (Lt. K. Campbell wounded).

1800 hrs. All officers of Right Coy. had now become casualties and Lt. F. Anson, M.C., was sent up to take over command with orders to clear the M.G's out of houses on the St. Aubert – Gommegnies Rd. These were found to be strongly held and the operation was repeated at 2200 hrs. successfully. Total casualties were: Killed—2 officers, 15 other ranks; Wounded— 4 officers, 91 other ranks; Missing—3 other ranks. (PRO: WO95/1219).

p. 197 Lt. A. H. S. Adair, M.C., wounded in action, 4th November 1918.

Peter T. Scott
November, 1988